Urban Homeownership

Published in cooperation with The Urban Institute, Washington, D.C.

Urban Homeownership

The Economic Determinants

Raymond J. Struyk
The Urban Institute

Assisted by
Sue A. Marshall

Lexington Books
D.C. Heath and Company
Lexington, Massachusetts
Toronto   London

Library of Congress Cataloging in Publication Data

Struyk, Raymond J.
    Urban homeownership.

    1. Home ownership—United States—Mathematical models. 2. House
buying—Mathematical models. 3. Housing—United States—Mathematical
models. I. Marshall, Sue A., joint author. II. Title.
HD7293.S78   643   75-27496
ISBN 0-669-00321-2

Published simultaneously in Canada.

Printed in the United States of America.

International Standard Book Number: 0-669-00321-2

Library of Congress Catalog Card Number: 75-27496

Contents

List of Figures

List of Tables

Preface

This book brings together several strands of the analysis of the characteristics of homeownership and the economic causes for households becoming homeowners. This work focuses primarily on the "demand side" of the tenure choice decision. It has only incidentally studied the amount of housing services consumed by homeowners as compared to renters; and, except in the conceptual discussion, it ignores the behavior of homeowners as suppliers of housing services. We are currently engaged in comparative econometric analyses of the behavior of landlords and homeowners as suppliers of housing services.

A number of individuals have generously contributed to this work. Frank de Leeuw provided the initial suggestion to study tenure choice and throughout the period of the study has provided incisive ideas and patiently read drafts of the individual chapters and the complete manuscript. Larry Ozanne, Victoria Lapham, and Heather Ross read parts of the manuscript and provided valuable criticisms. Mort Isler, Bob Tinney, and Cynthia Thomas all contributed through discussions of various general and technical problems. Dennis Eisen helped with some of the mathematics. Ray Fryer skillfully drafted many of the figures, and Sandra Simpson competently typed the manuscript. We are grateful for the assistance of all these people.

The research forming the basis for this publication was conducted pursuant to a contract with the Department of Housing and Urban Development. The views expressed are those of the authors and do not necessarily represent the views of The Urban Institute or of the Department of Housing and Urban Development.

Finally, we wish to note material which has been taken from prior publications. We have excerpted quotations or data from: John F. Kain and J.M. Quigley, "Housing Market Discrimination, Home Ownership and Savings Behavior," *American Economic Review*, 1972 (copyright 1972 by the American Economic Association); J.C. Weicher and J.M. Simonson, "Recent Trends in Housing Costs," *Journal of Economics and Business*, 1975 (copyright 1975 by Temple University); and, Henry J. Aaron, *Shelters and Subsidies* (copyright 1972 by the Brookings Institution). In addition we have made use of our own earlier work: "Income and Urban Home Ownership," *The Review of Economics and Statistics*, 1975 (copyright 1975 by the President and Fellows of Harvard College); "Estimation of Permanent Household Income Using the 1970 Census Users' File," 1975 (copyright 1975 by Temple University); "The Determinants of Household Home Ownership," *Urban Studies*, 1974 (copyright 1974 by *Urban Studies*); and, "Determinants of the Rate of Home Ownership of Black Relative to White Households," *Journal of Urban Economics*, 1975 (copyright 1975 by Academic Press, Inc.). Use of all of the above material is with permission of those holding the copyright.

1

Introduction

In the past decade the study of the economics of urban housing has been dominated by three issues, which in many ways have reflected the relatively recent interest in the subject. The first study area has been of the income and price elasticities of the household demand for housing services and of the price elasticity of supply, initially of new units and more recently of existing dwellings.[1] The second area of analysis has been of the intra-urban location of households and the variation in the price per unit of housing services; such analysis, associated with Richard Muth, Lowden Wingo, and William Alonso, has extensively developed a theory to explain differences in the spatial context of the city and have contributed much to understanding the functioning of the urban housing market.[2] The third area has dealt with several dimensions of the issue of race in urban housing markets. Lapham distinguishes three broad but related categories in the race and housing problem:[3] (a) the extent of residential segregation and its consequences, including job opportunity implications, (b) the differential price per unit of housing services faced by blacks and whites, and (c) whether racial segregation and/or white discrimination (if it exists) have affected the quantity or type of housing consumed by blacks.

A remarkable aspect of the enormous amount of research done on the areas just enumerated is the comparatively slight attention which has been paid to the way in which tenure—that is owning or renting the dwelling which the household occupies—impacts on these issues. While estimates of the price and income elasticities of demand have been calculated separately for owner-occupants and renters, this has resulted more from data availability and the need for checks on the consistency of the estimates than from explicit interest in the differences by tenure. The behavior of owner-occupants as suppliers of housing services is empirically unexplored. The spatial models of urban areas have not differentiated tenure,[4] and in the current generation of urban housing market simulation models it has not received a high priority.[a] Finally, with respect to the racial issue it is only very recently that lower rates of homeownership by urban blacks not associated with lower incomes was carefully observed, not to say under-

[a]The NBER and The Urban Institute models are the most fully developed and applied simulation models of urban housing markets. In their initial prototypes tenure choice is excluded. However, a version of The Urban Institute model which provides a distinction by tenure in the consumption of housing has been developed. Gregory Ingram, J.F. Kain, and J. Royce Ginn, *The Detroit Prototype of the NBER Urban Simulation Model* (New York: National Bureau of Economic Research, 1972). Frank de Leeuw, and R. Struyk, *The Web of Urban Housing* (Washington, D.C.: The Urban Institute, 1975).

stood. In brief, little systematic analysis of the economics of urban homeownership has been completed to date, especially when contrasted with the analysis of other aspects of urban housing. Given the lack of analysis, it is hardly surprising that there is a comparative void in our knowledge of this aspect of the economics of housing markets in urban areas.

Possession of such knowledge, though, could be instrumental in the development of incisive policies for the amelioration of housing and housing-related problems in our nation's cities. Consider the following as an example. If from other sources one knew that the ownership of dwellings by the individuals living in them resulted in a significantly greater degree of neighborhood stability (i.e., less turnover) and improved maintenance of the dwellings and properties, then it might be advantageous under certain conditions for homeownership to be encouraged in specific geographic areas. Such conditions might exist when (a) an area is anticipated to deteriorate at a moderate rate with widespread abandonment of a probable final outcome and (b) the housing stock in the same area is of sufficient quality as to make its withdrawal from the available stock socially wasteful and economically inefficient in a perspective broader than the individual units involved. To attempt to design a program to create a proper incentive to encourage ownership, it is necessary to know the degree of responsiveness of households of differing ages and compositions to price reductions or income inducements. At the present time extremely little is known about the economics of the household decision to own or rent the dwelling it occupies.

In another vein, there is a large variation in the rate of homeownership among metropolitan areas, among household types, and between blacks and whites (see Chapter 2 for documentation). It is of more than passing interest to discern the causes of such variation, to know whether the observed variations arise simply from differences in the preferences of households in different parts of the country or from differences in household types or race, or whether the variations represent responses to differences in the economic circumstances of individual households or the housing markets in which they are located. Being able to distinguish among the competing hypotheses is essential for informed policy judgments. Serious analysis of the effects of suspending some or all of the federal income tax advantages would, for example, rest on quantitative knowledge of the causal relationships just noted.

The purpose of this volume is to report the results of a careful consideration of the economic determinants of household homeownership with special emphasis on the role of the household's income in this decision. The research has focused on providing a thorough theoretical and empirical analysis of the income-tenure choice relationship.

One can define three broad classes of determinants of the tenure choice decision: (1) those associated with the household itself, (2) those which the household actively examines in making the tenure decision but which are not associated with individual households, and (3) those market conditions which the household accepts as given and in consequence does not study in making the tenure decision.

For the present purposes the household has several important characteristics. Foremost in the present analysis is its income. Because the purchase price of a dwelling is so large, nearly always requiring mortgage payments for a number of years, and because large transaction costs are associated with purchase or sale, both a household's current income and expected future income are relevant to the tenure decision. Other household characteristics of importance include its size and composition, i.e., the presence of children of various ages, the presence of an elderly relative, etc.; the age of the husband and wife or individual; and the occupations, skills, and education of its members.

When selecting a dwelling and form of tenure the household seeks information of several kinds. Of greatest concern is the price of housing bundles—a comparable bundle under both tenure forms and many bundles under each. In addition it may be necessary for the household to seek information on restrictions to locations and associated housing, especially in the case of minority group households.

The third set of determinants is really the factors which are reflected in the price per unit of housing services: the price of housing services overall; the degree of racial segregation and discrimination; the characteristics of the housing stock (the age distribution and the distribution by structural type, etc.), the size of the metropolitan area; the distributions of household incomes; and the distribution of households by family type, e.g., single individuals vs. young families. Beyond these factors are others, again ultimately reflected in prices, which contribute to the housing milieu in an area—that is, contribute to certain stylistic characteristics and to homeownership being clearly associated with "high quality" housing. The particular environment in an area stems from differences in the ownership tradition resulting partially from the ethnicity of the groups present at the time of the development of the modern city. It is also closely tied to the time of development through the then-current state of transportation and building technology. This milieu while often captured indirectly in economic analysis is a special force which has frequently been overlooked in establishing the market context.

All three sets of factors are of obvious importance in assessing the likelihood of a particular household purchasing its home in a particular metropolitan area. The problem of distinguishing between the "household effects" and the "area or market effects" has in part produced the adopted research strategy. Two separate empirical analyses, each with its own underlying theoretical model, have been carried out. In the first the unit of observation is the household but the sample is drawn entirely from a single housing market. In this way much of the confounding of household and area effects is avoided. The problem of households of different races or even households of different types facing different housing prices, both absolutely and the relative prices as owner-occupants and renters, are also eluded by estimating separate models for individual household types by race. A second reason for the analysis of households in a single market, though, is to obtain insights into the basic income-tenure choice relation. Knowledge of the functional form of this relationship at the household level is prerequisite for properly modeling the same relationship for groups of households in more aggregate analysis.

In the second analysis, the tenure choice of aggregates of households across metropolitan areas is studied. Here the variance in the rate of homeownership among cities for specific household types is related to the variation in the distributions of income and other characteristics of the household type and to the variance in the housing market conditions among cities, the market conditions being the third set of factors enumerated earlier. It is in this analysis that the effect on tenure choice of the conditions in the area in which the household lives are studied. Such conditions include variation in the relative price of owner-occupied housing services to black households and in the extent of racial discrimination in the residential sector to the degree that it is reflected in the available data.

Before proceeding further some note might be made of several broad limitations of the analyses presented in this volume. The analyses are dominantly economic in nature, which reflects the predilections and convictions of the authors. The work has also been restricted to the use of secondary data sources. For a combination of these reasons no explicit consideration is given to household attitudes toward homeownership nor the history or development of such attitudes (e.g., Did your family own its home when you were a child?). Further the study is one of statistical regularity and not of individual cases. Likewise, the role of institutions—lending institutions, poverty agencies, local governments, national government—in affecting the tenure decision is generally ignored, except to the degree to which the effects of their operations are embodied indirectly in the estimated coefficients. In brief, this study of tenure choice develops theoretical models of the economics of the tenure decision and then statistically tests the hypotheses encompassed in the models.

The remaining six chapters of the volume constitute three separate parts. Part I, consisting of Chapters 2 and 3, provides a general background material for the more specific analysis presented in the other parts. Chapter 2 provides some basic data on urban homeownership: the characteristics of owner-occupants and the variation in the rate of ownership among metropolitan areas. It also shows the dominance of the single-unit structure among homeowners and gives some data on the trends in homeownership over the past twenty years. The following chapter develops a broad conceptual model of the determinants of the decision to become an owner-occupant, which serves as a unifying device for the more limited theoretical models developed and applied in the second part. In the general model the frequency of ownership in an area is determined jointly with the average quantity of housing services consumed by owners and renters and the quantity of housing stock held by owner-occupants; the price per unit service of owner-occupied and rental housing services and the price per unit of the housing stock are also simultaneously determined with the frequency of homeownership. This conceptual model reveals some of the complexities underlying the less complete models which are estimated in the second part. It also serves as a valuable introduction to the factors involved in the tenure decision.

Part II presents specific models of the determinants of tenure choice which are econometrically estimated. The estimates in these chapters are the core of the analysis. Chapter 4 focuses on the decision of the individual household by analyzing the determinants of homeownership for households in the Pittsburgh metropolitan area. The analysis is conducted using separate samples for each household type for blacks and whites in order to rigorously test whether the determinants are quantitatively equivalent across these subgroups of the population of households. Chapter 5 analyzes the frequency of homeownership across metropolitan areas. An aggregate theoretical model is developed which has a direct household analog, and this model is estimated for several household types and for black and white households separately.

Part III utilizes the specific models and estimates of the preceding part to analyze selected policy issues. Chapter 6 addresses the reasons for the lower rates of homeownership of black households compared to white households of equivalent incomes. The aggregate tenure choice model developed in Chapter 5 is extended for the analysis, and econometric estimates of relative homeownership rates of black households to white households are made. The meaning of these results in terms of the actual happenings in a housing market are discussed and some immediate policy implications drawn. The major conclusion of this analysis is that increments to the average income of black households would be more powerful in achieving parity than would equivalent decrements to the price of owner-occupied housing which black households face. The examination of the composition and stability of the incomes of black families reveals that black husbands on average suffer greater rates of unemployment than do white husbands and that the earnings of wives in black families constitute a greater portion of total family income than white wives' earnings do in their families. Both of these factors work on average to require black families to have greater incomes than their white counterparts to obtain mortgage financing due to the discounting of womens' earnings and unstable earnings by lending institutions.

Chapter 7 uses the estimates made in Chapter 5 to evaluate the consequences on homeownership rates of a proposed national housing allowance program and of an increase in the price of owner-occupied housing services relative to rental services. These two phenomena were chosen both for their topical interest and to illustrate the range of issues which could be addressed using the econometric results developed in this volume.

Housing allowances—a national system of cash grants to the poor, earmarked in some way to be largely spent on housing—are found to produce only modest effects on the rate of homeownership of participating households, under the market conditions assumed for the analysis. A national program in which the poorest 22 percent of urban households would be eligible is estimated on net to shift about 210 thousand households to owner-occupant tenure, with the majority of those shifting from rental tenure being the lowest income households for whom the cash grants would be the greatest.

In examining the effects of increases in factor prices which cause the price (per unit of service) of owner-occupied housing to rise relative to the price of rental housing, a distinction is made between short-run and long-run consequences. The short-term consequences of increases, say in mortgage interest rates and land prices, falls on the marginal purchaser, especially those households wishing to purchase their first home. The reduction in the rate of home purchase for young, husband-wife families resulting from the acceleration in homeownership cost between 1967 and 1973 is estimated to be substantial; for families with 1970 incomes of $10,000, the reduction is about 20 percent. Over a longer time period, when the higher factor prices apply to all housing producers and homeowners, the effects of higher factor prices on the aggregate rate of homeownership is estimated to be quite modest; for households with a 1970 income of $10,000 the reduction is only about 2 percent—or probably less than could be caused by shifts in household preferences for owner-occupancy or by shifts in household composition.

Part I:
Numeric and Conceptual
Foundations

2 Basic Numbers on Urban Homeownership

The purpose of this chapter is simply to establish some notions of the rate of ownership in metropolitan areas and to describe a few of the more important ways in which rates of ownership vary among the population of urban households. The presentation is in three parts. In the first, the ownership patterns just described are documented for households in all American metropolitan areas (Standard Metropolitan Statistical Areas—SMSAs) combined. The second part of the chapter documents the variation among SMSAs in the rate of homeownership and the characteristics of owner-occupants. The final part examines the dominance of single unit structures among owner-occupant households and presents some data on the quantity of housing consumed by owner-occupant and renter households.

The Overall Picture

Who is likely to be an owner-occupant in metropolitan areas? There are four household characteristics which intuitively come to mind in response. Ownership seems likely to vary by (1) household type, i.e., husband-wife families versus others, and by the point of the household in the life cycle; (2) the income of household, since it often requires substantial resources for the initial costs of owning a home; (3) the race of household, which may largely reflect differences between races in household income; and (4) the size or number of persons in the household. In the following, ownership rates are related to each of these characteristics separately. Multivariate analysis appears in later chapters.

Table 2-1 provides substantial detail on the variation in homeownership by household type and by race for 1970. The data are organized in two ways. The first three columns show the distribution of ownership by household type *among owner-occupants*. These data shed light on the issue of which household types are dominant among owner-occupants. The second set of data, in the final three columns, shows the rate of homeownership for each household type.

Looking first at the distribution of ownership among owner-occupant households (col. 1-3), one is struck by the importance of husband-wife owner-occupants. For non-white households about two-thirds of the owner-occupants are in such households, while for white households it is nearly 80 percent. Since the distribution among owner-occupants to a certain degree simply reflects the distribution of all households, the data in the second set of

9

Table 2-1
The Pattern of Homeownership in Metropolitan Areas

Household Type	Distribution of Homeownership Among Households			Rates of Homeownership by Household Type by Race		
	Black & White	Black	White	Black & White	Black	White
Husband-wife families head	.783	.659	.791	.690	.503	.709
Under age 25	.018	.017	.018	.221	.156	.228
Age 25-34	.135	.110	.137	.553	.342	.574
Age 35-44	.190	.170	.191	.766	.549	.786
Age 45-65	.340	.290	.344	.795	.634	.816
Age 65 and over	.100	.082	.101	.739	.617	.749
Other Male-headed families, head	.031	.050	.030	.484	.365	.504
Under age 65	.024	.040	.023	.448	.346	.466
Age 65 and over	.007	.010	.007	.662	.487	.690
Other Female-headed families, head	.077	.164	.071	.440	.261	.497
Under age 65	.057	.131	.052	.393	.235	.451
Age 65 and over	.020	.033	.019	.660	.517	.684
Single individuals	.107	.124	.107	.354	.230	.541
Under age 65	.050	.078	.049	.279	.192	.642
Age 65 and over	.057	.046	.058	.466	.326	.478
All household types combined	1.00	1.00	1.00	.595	.385	.620

Source: U.S. Bureau of Census, Census of Housing, *1970 Metropolitan Housing Characteristics*, Final Report HC(2)-1, United States and Regions (Washington, D.C.: U.S. Government Printing Office, 1972), Tables B-7 and B-17.

columns are of greater interest. The highest rates of homeownership are attained for both races for the three husband-wife family categories with heads over age thirty-four. For younger husband-wife families ownership rates are much lower. This overall pattern is consistent with a simple life cycle model which posits a close relation between the timing of ownership and the presence in the family of children beyond the infancy stage. At this point in life the household has also often been able to assemble the capital required for home purchase. The rates of ownership are substantially lower for the other household types. For all household types headed by persons over age sixty-five the rate of ownership is remarkably high: about half of the elderly non-husband-wife black households are owner-occupants as are nearly 70 percent of the white households.

The data on rates of ownership point out the substantial differences between the rates of owner-occupancy between black and white households. Overall about 38 percent of black households and 62 percent of white households live in homes they own. For every family type the rate of ownership of whites exceeds that for blacks, although in general the two races demonstrate the same life cycle phenomena.

Some greater appreciation of the differences in ownership between the races can be gotten from Figure 2-1 which depicts the relation between the frequency of homeownership and household income for all households combined by race for 1970. At every income level the rate of ownership of black households is less than that for white. So the explanation for differences in ownership rates between races must at least in part rest in non-income factors.[a]

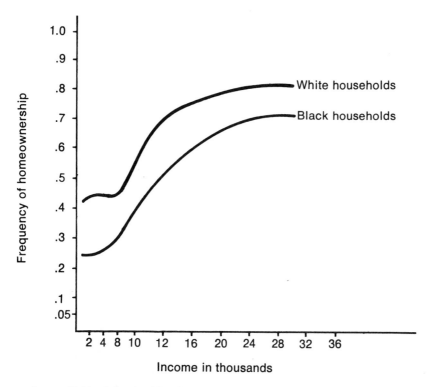

Source: Tables B-3 and B-13 U.S. Bureau of the Census, Census of Housing: *1970 Metropolitan Housing Characteristics* Final Report HC(2)-1, United States and Regions (Washington, D.C.: U.S. Government Printing Office, 1972).

Figure 2-1. Relation Between Frequency of Homeownership and Income for All Households by Race for All SMSAs for 1970

[a]Analysis of the rate of homeownership of black households relative to whites is the subject of Chapter 6.

Figure 2-1 also shows the aggregate relationship between the frequency of homeownership and household income to be non-linear. More specifically it shows that for those with little income and those with incomes over $20,000 the frequency of ownership is much less sensitive to increments of income than it is for the households whose income falls between these two groups. For moderate income households additional income is apparently a decisive factor in the decision to purchase a home; such additional income may, for example, make the crucial difference in getting the necessary credit rating or in being able to afford a home of the minimum desired size. For well-to-do households additional income makes little difference and the preferences for renter or owner tenure likely tell much of the story.

The final characteristic noted as a likely determinant of the decision to become an owner-occupant is the size of the household. Figure 2-2 graphs the aggregate relation between the frequency of owner occupancy and the number of persons in the household for husband-wife and other families separately by race. While there is a general increase in frequency of ownership with the number of persons in the household, the relationship is not consistent within the categories of households shown nor among them. This lack of a clear pattern should not be taken to indicate that household size is unimportant; it is probable that after the influence of income and other factors are controlled for statistically a clear relationship will be evident.

The above data have all been for 1970, the latest year for which such data are available from the decennial Census of Housing. Of considerable interest, though, are the 1970 homeownership rates in relation to those of the past two decades. Some evidence on the trend is displayed in Table 2-2. These data are based on all of the metropolitan areas with population of over 250,000 in 1960 for which we could obtain historical data (see Table 2-3). To ensure comparability over time, the 1970 SMSA boundaries as defined by the Bureau of the Census have been used in compiling the data for earlier years. The data show the average rate of homeownership for all households, the fraction of households headed by blacks, and the fraction of dwelling units in single unit structures.

Homeownership rose rapidly during the 1950s reflecting both pent up demand from the depression and war periods, and effects of federal legislation which greatly reduced the financial requirements for homeownership. During the 1960s, however, the trend turned downward. One possible explanation for this phenomenon could be the influx of black households with lower incidence of homeownership into major metropolitan areas; however, as the data show the portion of black households in major metropolitan areas increased uniformly over the 60s and the entire period. (For central cities, of course, the situation is dramatically different.) The reduction in demand for owner-occupancy is partly attributable to lower birthrates and later age at first marriage. Finally, rather interestingly, the fraction of dwelling units in the dominant owner-occupied structure-type—the single unit structure—increased slightly over the past decade

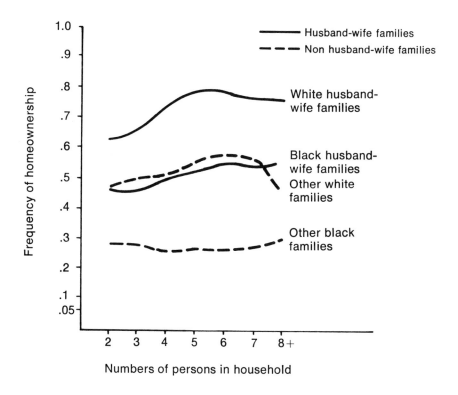

Source: Tables B-8 and B-18, U.S. Bureau of the Census, Census of Housing: *1970 Metropolitan Housing Characteristics* Final Report HC(2)-1, United States and Regions (Washington, D.C.: U.S. Government Printing Office, 1972).

Figure 2-2. Relation Between Frequency of Homeownership and Numbers of Persons in Household by Family Type by Race for All SMSAs for 1970

despite the downturn in the rate of homeownership. Thus the downturn was not produced by a shortage of the desired structure type.[1]

Variations Across Metropolitan Areas

That there is substantial variance in the rate of homeownership across metropolitan areas in the United States is readily apparent from the data in Table 2-4. These data are for the sample of thirty-nine metropolitan areas for which the Bureau of Labor Statistics collects data on the cost of housing services and

Table 2-2
Trends in Homeownership in Selected SMSAs, 1950-1970

	Year		
Variable	1950	1960	1970
Fraction of dwelling units owner occupied.	.537	.615	.579
Fraction of all households headed by blacks.	.095	.111	.122
Fraction of dwellings in one unit structures.	.550	.713	.729

other goods and services; this sample of cities is extensively used in the analysis presented later in this volume.[b]

The data in Table 2-4 are on a basis similar to those in Table 2-1. The final entries in the fifth and sixth columns show that while nearly 60 percent of all households in these areas are owner-occupants and roughly two-thirds of the areas fall in the 52-67 percent range, the extreme values are about 40 and 76 percent. The data in these columns also indicate that the total variance among urban areas in owner-occupancy rates is largely determined by three of six family types shown: young husband-wife families, non-husband-wife or "other" families, and primary individuals. Or conversely, there is relatively little variance

[b]A crude idea of comparability of the housing characteristics of the metropolitan areas included in the BLS data with all SMSAs is available from the mean of a number of such characteristics as of 1960 recorded below:

	Mean	
Characteristic	BLS SMSAs	All SMSAs
Percentage of dwelling units		
—owner occupied	50.8	59.3
—in single unit structures	70.0	66.6
—built '50-'60	31.0	31.7
—built '40-'50	16.1	16.6
—deteriorated	10.3	13.0
—delapidated	3.3	4.2
—without hot running water	5.0	5.3
—without tub/shower for exclusive use	7.8	7.7
Percentage of population non-white	11.8	10.8
No. of occupied units (000)	532	331

While the means are remarkably similar it is expected that the underlying distributions differ significantly, given the inclusions of the most populous SMSAs in the BLS data which over represents them relative to all SMSAs.

Table 2-3
Metropolitan Areas Included in Time Series Analysis

Akron	Miami
Albany-Schenectady-Troy	Milwaukee
Anaheim-Santa Ana	Minneapolis-St. Paul
Atlanta	New York
Baltimore	Newark
Birmingham	Norfolk
Boston	Oklahoma City
Buffalo	Paterson-Clifton-Passaic
Chicago	Philadelphia
Cincinnati	Phoenix
Cleveland	Pittsburgh
Columbus	Portland, Oregon
Dayton	Providence
Dallas	Rochester
Denver	Sacramento
Detroit	St. Louis
Fort Worth	San Antonio
Gary-Hammond	San Bernardino
Hartford	San Diego
Honolulu	San Francisco
Houston	San Jose
Indianapolis	Seattle
Jersey City	Syracuse
Kansas City	Tampa
Los Angeles-Long Beach	Toledo
Louisville	Washington, D.C.
Memphis	Youngstown

among areas in the owner-occupancy rates of the husband-wife family types with heads over age thirty.

The large differences among the family types both in total and for blacks and whites considered separately observed in the previous section are also evident in these data (columns 1 and 3). A more rigorous test of the mean differences in tenure rates by family types of the same race has been made using a student's t-test, and the results are recorded in Table 2-5. The calculated t-values are shown; a value greater than 2.0 indicates the difference in the mean to be significant at the 5 percent level of significance. Only two differences are not significant at this level: for white households it is the difference between husband-wife family types with heads 30-44 and 65 and over; for black households it is for similar family types with heads ages 45-64 and 65 and over.

Table 2-4

Variance in Homeownership by Household Type and Race for Selected SMSAs in 1970[a]

Household Type	White		Black		Total	
	Mean[b]	Coeff. of Var.[c]	Mean	Coeff. of Var.[c]	Mean	Coeff. of Var.[c]
Husband-Wife Family						
Head under age 30	.287	25.7	.193	37.8	.277	26.0
Head age 30-44	.775	7.5	.566	19.0	.754	8.3
Head age 45-64	.826	6.9	.666	15.9	.811	7.3
Head age 65 and over	.771	11.0	.627	20.5	.758	10.9
Other Families	.500	17.2	.300	33.0	.452	16.8
Primary Individuals	.373	23.3	.245	42.4	.378	28.3
All Households	.626	20.0	.406	24.8	.599	12.3

[a]Included cities: Atlanta, Austin, Baltimore, Baton Rouge, Boston, Buffalo, Chicago, Cincinnati, Cleveland, Dallas, Dayton, Denver, Detroit, Durham, Hartford, Houston, Indianapolis, Kansas City, Los Angeles, Milwaukee, Minneapolis-St. Paul, Nashville, New York, Orlando, Philadelphia, Pittsburgh, St. Louis, San Diego, San Francisco, Seattle, Washington, Wichita.

[b]Unweighted Average.

[c]Coefficient of variation is defined as the (standard deviation *100)/mean.

A difference of possibly greater interest which can also be tested here is that between races for each household type, noted earlier. The differences in average tenure rate for all households for the thirty-nine BLS cities were tested using a t-test. The differences are highly significant for all six of the family types shown. While the reason for these differences is partially the subject of the analysis of the following chapters, some preliminary observations are relevant. One is the degree to which tenure rates tend to vary together across cities for both races, i.e., is a high-tenure city likely to be so for both whites and blacks. Shown in Table 2-6 are the simple correlation coefficients between the incidence of owner-occupant tenure of black and white households; all are significant at the 5 percent level.

The correlations indicate that while the tenure rates do tend to move together for the two races, especially for some of the husband-wife family types, the degree of association is far from perfect. This quality of fit was, of course, to be expected from the greater coefficients of variation for black households compared to whites for every household type, as shown in Table 2-4.

Finally, some indication of the change in the variation among metropolitan areas in the rate of owner-occupancy over time can be garnered from the summary data for the sample of fifty-five large SMSAs discussed in the previous

Table 2-5

Student *t* Statistics for Test of Difference in the Mean Incidence of Owner-Occupant Tenure of Six Household Type by Race, 1970

	Husband-Wife Families with Head Age				Other Families
	Under 30	30-44	45-64	65 and over	
A. White Households					
Husband-Wife Families					
Head 30-44	29.4				
Head 45-64	32.7	3.4			
Head over 65	24.4	.2	3.0		
Other families	10.6	14.9	17.8	12.6	
Primary Individuals	4.3	21.8	24.7	18.6	5.9
B. Black Households					
Husband-Wife Families					
Head 30-44	16.2				
Head 45-64	20.8	3.7			
Head over 65	16.5	2.0	1.3		
Other families	4.9	10.3	14.3	11.4	
Primary Individuals	2.3	12.1	16.0	13.0	2.1

section. Table 2-7 lists the standard deviations and the coefficients of variation for 1950, 1960, and 1970. Judging by the coefficients of variation of the rate of homeownership, these cities became more alike during the fifties and then diverged somewhat during the sixties. Note, though, that the standard deviation, a measure of absolute dispersion, remained virtually unchanged 1960 to 1970. In terms of both the fraction of units in single unit structures and the fraction of households headed by blacks, these SMSAs have converged steadily over the twenty-year period.[c]

In sum, even simple cross-tabulations and one-way analysis indicate important differences in homeownership rates associated with race, household income, and household type. Further, a cursory examination of the rates of owner-occupancy across metropolitan areas reveals substantial variance among areas by race and household type. The statistical analysis in Part II of this volume is focused on determining the economic causes for the variation in ownership rates among

[c]The variation in the importance of black households (relative to its mean) has remained several times that of the relative variation in ownership rates or in the fraction of units in single unit structures.

Table 2-6

Simple Correlations Between Homeownership Rates of Black and White Households, by Household Type, in 1970

Household Type	Correlation
All households	.579
Husband-wife families, head age	
under 30	.766
30-44	.597
45-64	.719
65+	.712
Other families	.376
Primary individuals	.640

Table 2-7

Historic Variation Across Major U.S. Cities

	Year		
Variable	1950	1960	1970
Fraction of dwelling units owner-occupied			
standard deviation	.107	.090	.094
coefficient of variation	19.9	9.8	15.5
Fraction of all households headed by blacks			
standard deviation	.089	.097	.085
coefficient of variation	93.6	87.4	69.7
Fraction of dwellings in one unit structures			
standard deviation	.193	.146	.135
coefficient of variation	35.1	20.4	18.5

households in the same housing market and among household types in different housing markets.

The Single-Unit Structure and the
Quantity of Housing Services

The dominant structure type among owner-occupants has traditionally been the single-unit structure, although the recent surge in condominiums may change this pattern significantly. Since single-unit dwellings are typically larger than apartments it makes sense to discuss structure type together with the quantity of services consumed by owner-occupants and renters. Table 2-8 presents some data on the association between single unit structures and owner-occupancy for the BLS cities. The data in column 2 make evident that in 1970 owner-occupancy corresponded roughly with the household occupying a single-unit structure.[d]

The data in columns 3 and 4 show the ratio of the percentage of all units in single family dwellings to the percentage of all units which are owner-occupied; this ratio thus indicates the degree to which the rate of owner-occupancy and the rate of single unit structures move together across cities. A ratio of greater than unity indicates an excess of single-unit structures relative to owner-occupants, implying that single units are on balance being rented; a ratio of less than unity means on balance that multi-unit structures are owner-occupied.[e] While the ratios are reasonably close to unity, they nevertheless exhibit a substantial degree of variation, even if one excludes New York and Honolulu as special cases. For 1960 the extreme values are 0.90 for Boston and 1.59 for Durham; for 1970 they are 0.83 for Boston and 1.41 for Bakersfield. So a substantial degree of "crossing over" is indicated, despite the dominance of the single unit structure. From 1960 to 1970 the ratio either remained constant or declined for every included SMSA and likewise slightly reduced the degree of dispersion. (For 1960 the coefficient of variation was 16.8, while in 1970 it fell to 12.7.) The decline was caused dominantly by a decline in the importance of single-unit structures over the decade as a great number of multi-unit apartments were built.[f]

The data in Table 2-8 provide general information on the structures inhabited by owner-occupants, but they disguise some important differences between races. The differences in owner-occupancy and the related type of dwelling occupied by white and black households can be appreciated from the data in Figures 2-3 and 2-4 for St. Louis as of 1970. The data for St. Louis seem to be fairly representative in this regard. In the figures households are divided by: (1) race, (2) income for each race, (3) tenure for each race, and (4) structure type for each race-income-tenure. They show that at all three income levels black owner-occupants have chosen multi-unit structures at substantially higher

[d]Because the data for single-unit structures are for all structures and that on owner-occupancy is only for occupied structures, it is possible that the ratios can be misleading to the extent that vacancies are not distributed in proportion to the tenure distribution of the occupied stock or if so distributed to the extent that the actual distributions vary among SMSAs. For example, if the stock of vacancies contains a disproportionate number of units which are available only for purchase, the fraction of owner-occupied units to all occupied would be smaller and the entire ratio larger than otherwise.

[e]The dominant form of owner-occupancy of multi-unit structures is for the owner to occupy one unit of the structure in which he acts as the landlord for the other units. Virtually no data on the importance of condominiums are available from the Census.

[f]Of the thirty-seven included SMSAs, in nineteen the incidence of owner-occupancy increased while in eighteen others it fell. There was no clear tendency toward equalization of owner incidence among cities evident in the changes.

The decline in importance of single-unit structures in the housing stock of these cities over the 1960-1970 decade contrasts sharply with the experience of the previous decade during which single-unit structures increased in importance in all but six of the areas.

Table 2-8
Owner-Occupancy and Single-Unit Structure Data for 1960 and 1970 for Selected SMSAs[a]

	Percentage Units Owner-Occupied (1970)	Percentage Owner-Occupied Units in Single Unit Structures (1970)	Ratio: Percentage Units Single-Family Structure to Percentage Owner-Occupied[b] (1970)	(1960)	Ratio: Percentage Units Single Structure Plus One-Half Duplexes to Percentage Owner-Occupied[b] (1960)
Northeast					
Boston	52.6	77.9	.83	.90	1.07
Buffalo	62.9	79.5	.87	.91	1.13
Hartford	59.0	89.2	.95	.99	1.16
Lancaster, Pa.	68.9	89.1	1.09	1.26	1.30
New York City	36.8	70.3	.77	.85	1.04
Phil.-N.J.	67.1	94.3	1.08	1.12	1.16
Pittsburgh	67.8	90.3	1.05	1.16	1.23
Portland	60.6	86.7	.93	.93	1.12
North Central					
Chicago-Gary	52.9	81.6	.88	.92	1.05
Cincinnati	61.0	91.0	.99	.99	1.13
Cleveland	62.4	87.3	.94	1.01	1.14
Dayton	66.4	94.1	1.13	1.21	1.25
Detroit	72.1	90.8	.98	1.05	1.13
Green Bay	73.2	91.7	1.01	1.07	1.17
Indianapolis	65.4	92.0	1.10	1.22	1.26
Kansas City	65.7	93.2	1.09	1.11	1.16
Milwaukee	59.8	83.9	.92	.96	1.18
Minn.-St. Paul	65.2	91.9	.97	1.00	1.08
St. Louis	64.6	90.0	1.02	1.08	1.18
Wichita	64.7	91.4	1.20	1.22	1.26

South

Atlanta	57.5	94.0	1.19	1.24	1.30
Austin	54.9	92.8	1.26	1.40	1.44
Baltimore	58.2	92.9	1.20	1.22	1.29
Baton Rouge	66.4	95.3	1.19	1.33	1.37
Dallas	60.0	94.7	1.17	1.26	1.31
Durham	53.9	92.0	1.28	1.59	1.72
Houston	60.1	94.7	1.23	1.29	1.32
Nashville	62.2	91.5	1.14	1.24	1.32
Orlando	69.7	91.4	1.12	1.23	1.32
Washington, D.C.	46.0	95.8	1.17	1.21	1.24

West

Bakersfield	59.5	91.5	1.41	1.52	1.54
Denver	61.5	91.5	1.10	1.22	1.28
L.A.-Long Beach	48.5	91.7	1.26	1.25	1.29
San Diego	56.4	88.8	1.22	1.28	1.32
S.F.-Oakland	51.6	91.2	1.13	1.16	1.23
Seattle-Everett	64.9	93.4	1.09	1.13	1.15
Honolulu	40.7	89.2	1.14	1.67	1.76

[a]The 37 included SMSAs are among the 39 for which the Bureau of Labor Statistics gathers housing cost data.

[b]Percent owner-occupied units are based on only occupied units; percent single unit structures are based on all units.

Sources: 1960 and 1970 *Census of Housing*.

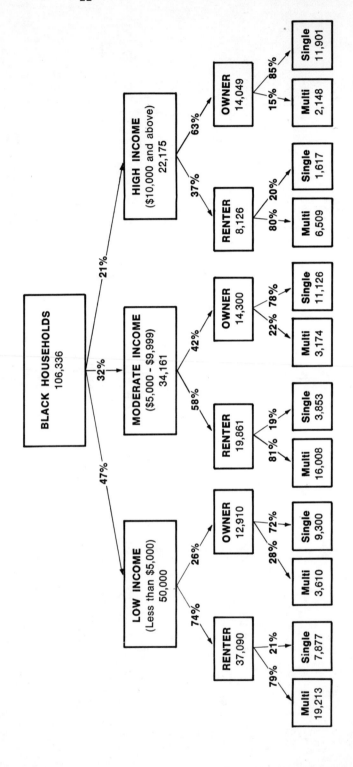

Source: R.F. Kirby et al., "Residential Zoning and Equal Housing Opportunities: A Case Study in Black Jack, Missouri," Paper 712-8-1, Washington, D.C., The Urban Institute, 1972, Table 1.

Figure 2-3. Black Households in the St. Louis SMSA, 1970, by Income, Tenure, and Housing Structure Type

23

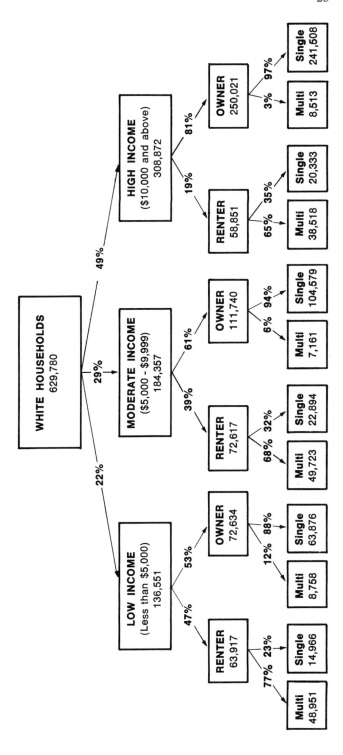

Source: R.F. Kirby et al., "Residential Zoning and Equal Housing Opportunities: A Case Study in Black Jack, Missouri," Paper 712-8-1, Washington, D.C., The Urban Institute, 1972, Table 2.

Figure 2-4. White Households in the St. Louis SMSA, 1970, by Income, Tenure, and Household Structure Type

rates than whites. This phenomenon likely results not from a preference of blacks for these units but from the segregation of black households into the older centralized portions of metropolitan areas where multi-unit structures dominate. For the moment, however, only note the marked differences between the races.

As a final matter, some broad indications of the quantity of housing services consumed by owner-occupants and renters are given. The most comprehensive measure, of course, would be the expenditures by households. The determination of comparable expenditures for owner-occupants and renters is beset by a number of difficulties. For example, ratios of rents to values have been found to differ widely among metropolitan areas, structural characteristics of dwellings, and locations within metropolitan areas.[2] Because of these problems monthly "rents" have been computed for owner-occupied units using three different values of the average ratio of rents to house values (0.006, 0.008, and 0.01). Other work suggests 0.008 to be the best overall average estimate of the ratio, with higher values probably more appropriate for older units and lower values for newer units. Using a rent-value ratio of 0.008, owner-occupants are computed on average to consume about 18 percent more housing; in terms of number of rooms (also shown in Table 2-9,) they consume 27 percent more housing than renters.

A point of some interest is that for relatively low levels of household income, say under $5,000 annually, the consumption of housing by owner-occupants and renters is indicated by these data to be quite similar. At higher income levels owner-occupants consume more, and it is the increasing incidence of homeownership with higher incomes which produces the greater overall consumption by owner-occupants. Based on these data one might conjecture that the greater consumption by owner-occupants is due to the lower price they pay for housing due to considerable tax advantages of homeownership; this subject is pursued as part of the analysis which follows.

Table 2-9

Measures of Quantity of Housing Services Consumed by Owner-Occupant and Renter Households in Metropolitan Areas by Income Class, 1970

Income Class ($000)	Monthly "Rents"				Number of Rooms	
	Owner-Occupants					
	$R/V =$ .006[a]	$R/V =$ .008[a]	$R/V =$ .01[a]	Renters	Owner-Occupants	Renters
Under 2	41	55	69	60	3.22	3.10
2-3	42	55	69	60	3.24	3.12
3-4	42	56	70	63	3.28	3.15
4-5	43	57	71	65	3.34	3.18
5-6	43	58	72	69	3.40	3.20
6-7	44	59	73	73	3.48	3.23
7-10	48	64	80	81	3.73	3.30
10-15	64	85	107	100	4.29	3.44
15-25	102	136	170	127	4.99	3.56
Over 25	185	247	309	159	5.57	3.52
All Households	73	97	121	82	4.21	3.31

[a]R/V is the ratio of gross rents to house value as reported by the Census. "Rents" for owner-occupants are the product of (R/V) and the value of the home which the household reports. The value of 0.008 is probably the best overall estimate of this ratio. Lower values (e.g., 0.006) are applicable to newer than average homes with their greater expected life, and higher values (e.g., 0.01) to homes older than average. For more on the variance in rent/value ratios see R. Struyk and Sue Marshall, "Regional Variation in Housing Attribute Prices," *Northeast Regional Science* 4 (1974): 51-59.

Source: Tabulations of data on Tables B-1 and B-2 in U.S. Bureau of the Census, Census of Housing 1970 *Metropolitan Housing Characteristics* (Washington, D.C.: U.S. Government Printing Office, 1972).

3

A General Framework

Much of the past work on tenure choice has been characterized by an inadequate conceptual basis and understanding of both the choice of tenure and the consumption of housing services under a given tenure form. The present chapter seeks to establish a general conceptual framework within which the more specific and rigorous models of tenure choice which are developed in the later chapters can be placed.

The chapter consists of two separate but related sections. In the first the housing consumption and tenure choice decisions of individual households are discussed in detail, and the general tenure choice model used in later chapters is developed. The second section focuses on the aggregate tenure and consumption decisions within metropolitan areas. Based on the analysis of the individual household decisions, a model is developed which treats the markets for owner-occupied and rental services as interdependent as well as specifying the tenure and consumption decisions as jointly determined. In both analyses it is assumed that individual housing markets are in long-run equilibrium; the requisite model, then, is comparatively static in nature; in this setting the explicitly dynamic aspects of the adjustment process are ignored.

Tenure Choice and Housing Consumption by Individual Households

In this section three partial models are developed. The first two are of the behavior of renters as consumers of housing services and of owner-occupants as consumers and investors as well as their own landlords. The purpose of the models is to draw out the implications of the tenure decision itself for household behavior. The final model is of the tenure choice itself. In this model the effects of the differential behavior of renters and owner-occupants enter through the relative prices of owner-occupied and rental housing. The final part of this section presents a summary overview of the previous discussion which may be of particular interest to the less technically-oriented reader.

Housing Consumption

Owner-Occupants. Consideration of the housing consumption decision of an owner-occupant involves two highly-related decisions: (a) that concerning the

27

amount of housing services he demands for consumption, and (b) that concerning the amount of capital stock he demands as an investment. This means that the prices and quantities of housing services and the housing stock demanded need to be considered as jointly determined. A final consideration is the amount of services the owner-occupant provides himself from his stock.

Housing in this analysis is generally conceived as constituting a homogeneous commodity such that dwellings differ only in the quantity of services which they possess. More specifically it is assumed that there exists a set of weights which can convert the bundle of physical attributes to which consumers attach value into a quantity index. These attributes include the number of rooms, the amount and dependability of the heat provided by the heating system, and a pleasing architectural style, to name but a few components as illustrations. The important point for this analysis, though, is the ability to divide rents into a quantity of services and a price per unit of service components.[1]

Now turning to the demand for housing services, $Q_d{}^s$, it has traditionally been expressed as a function of permanent income, Y; family characteristics and point in the life cycle, *fam*; the price per unit of services, P_{so}; and the price of other goods, π.[2] There are two additional factors in this case. An additional price, the price of rental housing services, P_{sr}, is required as it is the price of the closest substitute. The second factor is the amount of housing stock which has been demanded for investment, $Q_d{}^k$. The proposition is that given some level of stock has been demanded and obtained for investment purposes, its availability may effect the observed $Q_d{}^s$. The household in question may actually be consuming more or less services than it would in the absence of the investment consideration. The demand for housing services can be written, then, as:

$$Q_d{}^s = f(Y, fam, P_{so}, P_{sr}, \pi, Q_d{}^k), \tag{3.1}$$

At the same time, though, it is evident that $Q_d{}^s$ likely enters into the determination of $Q_d{}^k$. One would expect at least that $Q_d{}^k$ would be great enough to provide services sufficient for the minimum living requirements of the family; it is much less easy to argue for $Q_d{}^s$ placing a maximum constraint on the level of investment since rooms could always be left unused, etc. Investment in any asset will also depend on its rate of return relative to those available from alternative investments. In light of these comments the demand for housing stock as an investment can be expressed as

$$Q_d{}^k = g[Q_d{}^s, r_o, r, W] \tag{3.2}$$

where r is the rate of return available on other investments and W is a measure of the family's wealth. r_o is the rate of return on the housing unit in question, exclusive of federal tax treatment of ownership-related deductions. It is related by the following identity to the price of services per unit, P_{so}, and the price of stock per unit, P_k:

$$r_o \equiv \frac{P_{so} - P_o}{P_k} - d \qquad (3.3)$$

where P_o is the price of operating inputs and d is depreciation. The relationship between wealth and $Q_d{}^k$ is likely to be dissimilar from that between wealth and other investments. Over a substantial range of wealth it can be expected that the only non-savings investment will be housing; after some threshold of wealth, portfolio diversification is initiated. In particular Bossons has identified three effects which portfolio balance considerations will have on the holdings of housing as an asset:[3]

1. As wealth increases the attainable trade-off between the consumption of services from owned housing stock and portfolio diversification will be eased. Diversification will tend to be dominated by the demand for owned services by households with low wealth, and the wealth elasticity of the share of assets held in the form of owner occupied housing should consequently be negative.
2. Household wealth may be divided into controlled financial assets (including housing), financial assets the disposition and allocation of which is controlled by others (e.g., pensions), and human capital. For households with a given total wealth, the relative inflexibility of financial assets controlled by others will cause the elasticity of ownership with respect to the portion of total wealth held in the form of assets controlled by others to be negative (holding total wealth constant) and to be positive but less than the elasticity with respect to controlled financial assets holding controlled assets constant.
3. For households whose controlled assets include business assets (e.g., equity in a closely held corporation), the relative illiquidity of business assets will cause the elasticity of owned houses with respect to business assets to be negative.

As the portfolio grows, more of most types of investments are held, and it seems reasonable that this applies to housing, although the elasticity is likely small. In simply including the level of wealth in the function for $Q_d{}^k$ a discontinuity in the relationship is anticipated at the point at which portfolio diversification begins.[a]

---

[a] The data and analysis by Projector and Weiss on the composition of wealth support this point. Wealth holdings are divided among the following classes by age of household head and size of wealth: own home, automobile, business and profession, liquid assets, investment assets, and miscellaneous. Wealth is defined on an equity basis in that debts (mortgages) secured by assets (homes) included in the wealth estimates were deducted from the values of the assets.

The data, aggregated over all income groups, on the share of wealth held in their own home and automobiles show a sharp reduction in the share of wealth in these assets occurring at levels of wealth estimated at over $25,000 in 1962. (Home and auto are combined because of some strong trade-offs between them at the lower levels of wealth.) The decline in the home-auto share is compensated mainly by various "business-profes-

A fundamental issue is how the owner-occupant's owning the housing stock affects the demand for services beyond the fairly direct "availability" effect already mentioned. Before pursuing this it should again be noted that under consideration at this stage of the discussion is the decision process of individual owner-occupants, not of individuals who are weighing the relative merits of this tenure form.

An economist quite naturally views the lower costs resultant from owner-occupancy which effect Q_d^s as a price effect. The most conspicuous element in the distortion of actual from nominal prices are those accruing through federal tax subsidies, i.e., the deductibility of property taxes and interest payments and the exclusion of imputed rents. There may, however, be other elements; one often asserted advantage of homeownership is lower per-unit maintenance costs, although this has not been documented. On the other side of the coin, there are some clear disadvantages to ownership, most notably the risk of various types of loss which are incurred. Such losses not only include outright destruction of the physical asset, but also loss from neighborhood deterioration. Most of these should be reflected in the rate of return and riskiness of the investment included in (3.2). The net effect of the federal tax subsidy on the housing consumption of an average household is described in Figure 3-1, a standard indifference curve diagram. The broken indifference curves and budget line refer to the situation faced by the household if it rents; the solid lines depict the situation if it is an owner-occupant. Note that the owner's budget line (B_o) should be increasingly concave as it approaches the horizontal axis which would reflect the greater subsidies per dollar of housing which are available as more housing is consumed.[4,5] As B_o is everywhere above B_r, it is evident that more housing services will be consumed by the owner-occupant with the fraction of marginal income spent on housing depending on the household's income elasticity of demand.

Thus a fundamental effect of homeownership is an increase in Q_d^s. The only adjustment required for the model to incorporate the effect of tax subsidies, S, is to replace P_{so} in (3.1) with SP_{so}, and to add a function determining the relation between the subsidy and income. The function determining the subsidy obtained by a given household can be written as[b]

---

sional" and investment assets. On the other hand, the calculation of the elasticity of homeownership (as a share of wealth) with respect to total wealth by class of total wealth indicates homeownership to be wealth elastic only to $10,000 for family heads under thirty-five and to $5,000 for older family heads. Again, however, sharp changes in the elasticities between wealth classes are noted. For a further description and analysis of the composition of wealth see D.S. Projector and G.S. Weiss, *Survey of Financial Characteristics of Consumers* (Washington, D.C., Board of Governors of the Federal Reserve System, 1966).

[b]Clearly, the price considered at the time of purchase would be appropriately discounted for whatever future changes the household may perceive as likely to occur with some certainty. Also, (3.4) likely overstates the tax advantages to homeownership since in the long run the accelerated depreciation allowed on rental property since 1954 should be reflected in lower rents. On this point see Aaron, "Income Taxes and Housing," and R. Slitor, *The Federal Income Tax in Relation to Housing* (Washington, D.C.: GPO, The National Commission on Urban Problems, 1968), Research Report No. 5, especially pp. 12-17 and the Appendix.

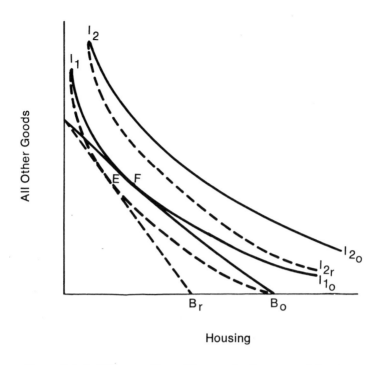

Figure 3-1. Indifference Curve Diagram for Owners and Renters

$$S = \beta_y (\gamma Q_d^s P_{so} + R_y)/P_{so} Q_d^s \qquad (3.4)$$

where β_y is the marginal tax rate for income level Y, γ is the fraction of housing expenditures qualifying for favorable tax treatment, and R_y is the imputed net rental income from the property equal to the rent value ratio times $P_k Q_d^k$. (A more complete discussion of tax advantages is given in Appendix B.)

A second possible behavioral difference of owner-occupants stems from their actions as their own landlords. It has been hypothesized by several researchers, for example, that neighborhoods with higher rates of homeownership are better maintained over time[6] especially in the face of serious shocks such as racial transition. If landlords are assumed to act rationally in these cases,[c] homeowners should be viewed as over-investing in their properties. To understand (and model) the behavior of the owner-occupant, his joint roles as consumer and supplier must be explored.

Given his tenure choice, the owner-occupant demands a certain level of

[c]Franklin James' study of the behavior of landlords in Newark suggests that in the face of racial transition in a neighborhood some apparently discriminating landlords do not act rationally under those circumstances. For details, see his "Housing Abandonment in Newark: Neighborhood Segregation, Landlord Discrimination, and the Abandonment of Rental Properties," New Brunswick, N.J., Rutgers Center of Urban Policy Research, processed, 1972.

housing services, as stated by (3.1). As his own landlord, however, the owner-occupant will seek to maximize his net revenue properly discounted so as to satisfy his simultaneous demand for a competitive return on his investment. In any market, price is determined by demand and supply factors; similarly, the individual owner-occupant exists within the overall housing market but at the same time establishes the price of housing services for himself since he controls both demand and supply. Quite obviously he must keep his price within the general bounds set by the market or he will suffer losses.

To amplify this last point, consider the owner-occupant who ostensibly over-improves an older house in a neighborhood of similar but less-well maintained homes. In terms of the present model what is happening can be seen from the following. First, we introduce a supply of services function, written in the price determining form for convenience.[d]

$$P_{so} = n(P_k, Q_d^s, P_o, E)$$ (3.5)

where E captures his expectations of the future flow of net rentals and his rate of time preference. Thus the owner-occupant's price to himself for services is based on the price of his investment, the costs of operating the unit, the amount of services demanded from the unit, and his expectations. In the case at hand, a greater level of Q_d^s is demanded; say the owner wanted a larger informal dining area adjacent to his kitchen which required a major remodeling job. P_{so} would have to rise as the owner-occupant moves up his supply curve; but as the landlord he must decide on expanding services as an investment decision.

The demand for additional services implies a demand for a greater stock, and there must be a supply schedule for the stock. One such supply function, again written in the price determining form, is

$$P_k = m(P_c, Q_d^k, M)$$ (3.6)

where P_c is the price of capital inputs. M is a vector a variables reflecting the market conditions for housing in general and for owner-occupied housing in particular; among these variables are the growth rate of the area and the attributes of the stock such as the distribution by structure type. The price of capital inputs varies with the financial reputation of the owner, the "quality" of

---

[d]An issue not raised in the text is the reason for the explicit inclusion of a supply function. If supply were highly price elastic, it would be unnecessary to take supply responses into account. However, recent estimates on the supply elasticity of rental housing services by de Leeuw ("The Supply of Rental Housing," *American Economic Review*, December 1971, pp. 806-17) suggest that the elasticity is rather low. Other researchers, such as R.F. Muth, "Demand for Non-Farm Housing," have argued that supply, especially of new dwellings, is highly price elastic. Given the likelihood of a non-highly elastic supply at least for services from existing dwellings, inclusion of an explicit function in this general framework seemed warranted.

the property, and so forth as well as general conditions in the market for loanable funds. Whether P_k is driven upward by the demand for capital depends on the price of capital for the improvement versus the initial price of capital. Assuming a rise in P_k, how far P_{so} rises depends ultimately on the price elasticity of demand for capital. From the rate of return identity (3.3), it is clear that whether the rate of return remains competitive depends on the magnitude of the changes in P_{so}, P_o, and P_k. In the case at hand, a reduction in the market's valuation of r_o (i.e., $d(p_{so} - p_o) < dP_k$) seems likely given the probable high cost of capital (P_c) for improvements, which generally take the form of a second mortgage. The owner-occupant may be able in the short run to disguise the decline in r_o by loaning himself the money and not accurately measuring its opportunity cost or by reducing P_o through sacrifice of leisure time, for example. In the long run, however, when he sells the dwelling the market's capitalization of net income will be the determining factor.

This scenario could, however, work out much differently. P_{so} rises as far as the interplay of demand and supply will allow. While most landlords would be unwilling to make an investment in a property located as this one is because of the uncertainty of future demand, the owner-occupant enjoys a distinct advantage here in being able to forecast his future demand with much greater certainty than the landlord. Hence, the investment may be a good one, even if the neighborhood deteriorates since the internal rate of return may be able to more than compensate for the capital losses. The owner-occupant as a supplier behaves perfectly rationally, if the price he is willing to pay as a consumer is high enough. The irrationality, if any, is on the part of the consumer.[7]

The various pieces of a model of the demand for and supply of housing services for an owner-occupant household can now be assembled. The four functions and two identities in the system are:

$$Q_d^s = f(Y, fam, SP_{so}, P_{sr}, \Pi, Q_d^k) \tag{3.7a}$$

$$Q_d^k = g[Q_d^s, r_o\ r, W] \tag{3.7b}$$

$$P_{so} = n(P_k, Q_d^s, P_o, E) \tag{3.7c}$$

$$P_k = m(P_c, Q_d^k, M) \tag{3.7d}$$

$$S = \beta_Y(\gamma(Q_d^s P_{so}) + R_y)/P_{so} Q_d^s \tag{3.7e}$$

$$r_o \equiv \frac{P_{so} - P_o}{P_k} - d \tag{3.7f}$$

Even cursory study of (3.7) makes evident the complexity of the determination of the owner-occupant's demand for housing services. This formulation also serves to emphasize the complex processes summarized by functions like (3.7a) which are typically subjected to empirical investigation.

Renters. The model of the determinants of the demand and supply of housing services by a household in the rental market has been formulated elsewhere and need not be reproduced in detail here.[8] The two important distinctions between the behavior of owners and renters are: (a) the decision on the quantity of housing services to rent is independent of direct investment considerations and (b) renters are price takers in the sense that owner-occupants are not, as just discussed. The demand function for a renting household is

$$Q_d = o\,(\,Y, fam, P_{sr}, P_{so},\, \pi\,). \tag{3.8a}$$

Note that there is no subsidy, S, in this function, although some tax subsidies due accrue to renters indirectly. (See Appendix B and note b.) The supply function faced by the renter is

$$P_{sr} = p\,(P_c, P_o, Q_d, M, E\,) \tag{3.8b}$$

Q_d enters with the idea of a renter asking for greater services from a given unit and the landlord responding by moving up his supply schedule; the market price per unit of service is, however, exogenous to the renter.

Tenure Choice

Thus far the models of demand for housing services by individual owner-occupants and renters have been formulated under the supposition that the tenure decision had already been made. While this offered a convenient starting point for the discussion, it is now time to remove this fiction and to explore the decision to become a homeowner.

In discussing the demand for housing services, it was both convenient and realistic to treat demand as a continuous phenomena. The foremost characteristic of the tenure decision, however, is its discrete nature: the unit is or is not owner-occupied. As a consequence, it is convenient to posit two functions for a household, one as a renter and one as an owner-occupant. Without explicitly stating these functions they can be assumed to be well-behaved; and the first order conditions for utility maximization can be stated: regardless of tenure form, the household maximizes its utility by equating the price weighted marginal utilities of the goods it consumes and by exhausting its income on utility yielding goods (including savings). This simple description of household behavior underlies the following statements.

If the price per unit of rented and owner-occupied housing services were identical and the quantity of housing services were the same under both forms of tenure, then a household will own its home if its utility as an owner-occupant exceeds that as a renter. If the price of housing services varies with tenure, though, the situation is less straightforward. Consistent with the previous discussion assume the price per unit of owner-occupied housing services to be less than the price of rental services, due to federal tax advantages to homeownership. Unless the *level* of utility from rental housing is much greater than that from owned, total utility of the household should be greater as an owner-occupant than as a renter, since it will be able to consume at least more housing and likely more of both goods (depending on income elasticities) as an owner-occupant. One would expect households to be owner-occupants, at least over that portion of the income distribution for which $P_{so} < P_{sr}$ due to tax advantages, preferred treatment by lending companies, and so forth.

Since owner-occupancy is not a certainty even at the highest income levels, it is important to ask what causes the level of utility from rented housing to be sufficiently greater than the level of utility from owned housing to offset the price advantage. The basic situation is depicted in Figure 3-1 in which the owner and renter indifference curves depicted by I_1 (or I_2) show an equivalent utility level. That is, even though a renter could consume more housing services at any level of other goods by becoming an owner-occupant, he may prefer not to and has as much utility from consuming relatively less housing as a renter as he would consuming more as an owner. In the diagram the difference in housing consumption is EF, with the household being in equilibrium as a renter at E.

Renters derive utility from lack of maintenance duties, avoidance of uncertainty and high transactions costs, and other phenomena which come with homeownership. This offers a partial explanation for differences in the utility levels by tenure, but more fundamental reasons are likely associated with family type, size, and composition as well as the household's income.[9] Also, owner-occupancy is very likely a "normal good" and as such should generally be more likely as income rises.

In formulating a model of the demand for owner-occupancy those phenomena just described as affecting the level of utility households derive from owning versus renting their dwelling should be included. Under the assumption of no constraints other than those already noted, a demand function for owner-occupancy can be expressed as

$$Q_o = b\,(\ln Y,\, fam,\, SP_{so},\, P_{sr},\, \pi,\, Q_d^{\,k}) \tag{3.9}$$

where Q_o is probability of a household choosing to own its home; income is expressed as the natural log of income only to note the nonlinearity of its relation with the probability of homeownership (as discussed below). The investment considerations aside from the tax subsidies are summarized in $Q_d^{\,k}$. The market conditions and other factors which define the situation within which the household makes its decision are accounted for by P_{sr}, P_{so}, and π; and the income and familial-life cycle factors are contained in the remaining term.

Of substantial importance, for both the current discussion and for the empirical work presented in the later chapters, is the relation between ownership and income. Figure 3-2 depicts graphically the discrete relationship between the probability of homeownership and income for a given household holding the family characteristics, its preferences, and market conditions fixed. Below some critical income level, k_i, the probability of ownership by the ith household is zero; above it, the probability is unity. Now, if one introduces additional households broadly similar to the ith except for income (e.g., nonelderly, married, white), two factors act to make the function continuous. First, even among households with the same level of income some stochastic variation is introduced which effectively makes k_i a locus of points instead of a single point. As an example, some households will have low- or no-down payment VA loans available to them. Second, one can allow one or more of the givens, such as family size, to vary and this in turn varies the position of k_i. The resultant relationship is likely to be similar to that shown in Figure 3-3 in which the probability of owning a home asymptotically approaches an upper bound (possibly unity) as the household's income becomes great enough. Further smoothing can be anticipated as one aggregates over households, as would be done in an analysis of variation in aggregate tenure across metropolitan areas.

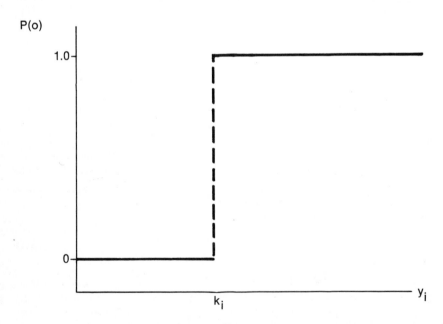

Figure 3-2. The Discrete Household Income-Tenure Relation

And, indeed, the ownership-income curve for an urban household in the United States given in Figure 2-1 is very similar to the curve in Figure 3-3.

Two summary points can be made here. First, the tenure decision function links the rental and owner-occupant markets on the demand side. Second, while it is not possible to simply add (3.9) to the model of owner-occupant demand for and supply of housing services shown in (3.7), the joint determination of the tenure decision and the demand for quantity of services decisions should be evident.

A Summary Overview

Many aspects of the behavior of owner-occupants as compared to renters in their demand both for housing services and the tenure choice itself can be captured by thinking of the effect which many market forces have on the price per unit of

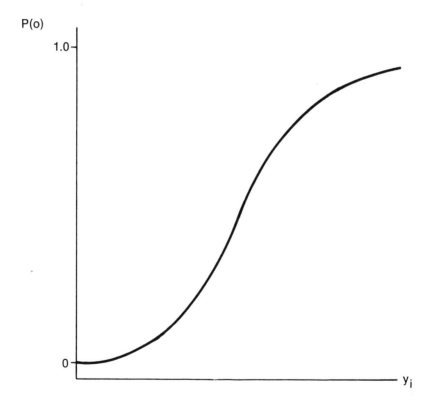

Figure 3-3. The Continuous Household Income-Tenure Relation

housing services confronted by the household depending on its tenure status. This can be rephrased in terms of the indifference curve diagram in Figure 3-4 which shows the various consumption possibilities of housing and all other goods and services. The figure is for an individual household and it depicts three different equilibria points—points which are combinations of housing and other goods which would maximize the household's utility or satisfaction under the constraints indicated by each of the three budget lines. For clarity the indifference curve themselves are omitted from the diagram.

Consider first the renter household. This household goes into the market and, given the price per unit of rental housing services, purchases that quantity of services which combined with the complimentary quantity of other goods maximizes its utility. The household is a price taker with respect to housing. In exchange for his rent the household receives generally duty-free housing services, including freedom of worry about maintenance and the safety of his investment. The household is also free to invest its money as it sees fit, even to keep it in a highly liquid savings account. In Figure 3-4 the budget constraint facing the renter is RR', and this household is in equilibrium at point a.

The situation of the renter contrasts sharply with that of the owner-occupant whose housing decisions are made under uncertainty and whose price per unit of housing services may exceed or be lower than those of his renting counterpart. That is, the owner's budget constraint might be RS or RT; and his housing consumption greater or less than the renter's at b or c, respectively.

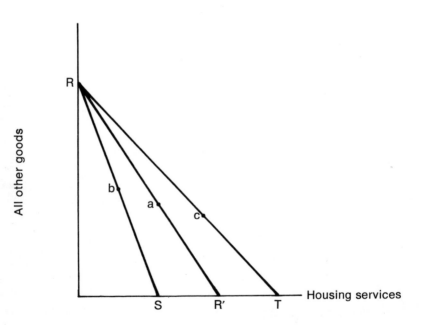

Figure 3-4. Renter and Owner-Occupant Budget Lines

What are the factors which determine the relative position of the owner's budget line? They fall broadly into four categories which are not mutually exclusive: (1) tax considerations, (2) investment and maintenance aspects, (3) market conditions, and (4) race. The first two conditions are associated with the individual household while the latter two are clearly beyond the ability of one household to affect. (Market conditions and race are discussed further in the next section.) As argued in Appendix B, the income tax advantages to homeownership probably dominate those potentially passed on to renters by landlords and make the price of owner-occupied services less than that of rental services.

The investment side of the picture is much less clear. The return on an investment in housing may or may not surpass that available from other alternatives; and, occasionally rapid neighborhood change makes it difficult to avoid capital losses. Further, for many households the purchase price of a home represents the majority of its assets and the mortgage payments constrain portfolio diversification and thus the reduction of risk. "Maintenance" refers really to the strategy of investment in upkeep and capital improvements followed by the household over time, i.e., after the purchase of the dwelling. Again, it is possible to invest too much or not enough so as to adversely affect the capital gains realized at time of sale. The budget line also refers to the comparative cost of maintaining a unit. For the owner-occupant who does not have a taste for doing much of the routine maintenance himself and who does not share a maintenance program with others as in a condominium, the cost of hiring work done can easily be greater than the cost of similar work on rented units where economies of scale are possible.

Market conditions refer to the rate of growth of the area, the availability of units especially suited for owner-occupancy, and so forth. When suitable units are in short supply, for example, the relative price of owner-occupancy will rise. Finally, with respect to race there is a growing body of evidence to support the hypothesis that owner-occupancy is more expensive for minority households. Such costs include not only higher purchase prices exacted by reluctant sellers but also higher search costs which are incurred in overcoming the poor information on units available outside of traditionally minority areas.

Thus the relative position of the rental and owner-occupant budget constraints depend on the household's income (through income tax rates and differential mortgage rates), its race, and its managerial skill in selecting and maintaining a dwelling unit. The relative prices of owner-occupied and rental housing services to a given household will not, however, fully determine its tenure choice. Different households have varying preferences for owner-occupancy and it is the strength of these preferences coupled with market prices which ultimately determine the households tenure choice as was demonstrated through the different indifference curves in Figure 3-1. Households with a preference for owner-occupancy will only be induced to be renters by lower rental housing prices, the extent of the required discount depending, of course, on the price elasticity of demand for owner-occupancy.

A Model of Aggregate Tenure Choice
and Housing Consumption

It is the burden of this section to augment and transform the basic relationships developed for individual households in the previous sections in sketching a model of aggregate tenure choice in a housing market. To accomplish this three tasks are required. First, the relation between the prices of rental and owner-occupied housing must be more tightly defined. Second, when examining an entire market some account must be taken of the possible effects of residential racial segregation and discrimination. Finally, aggregation across households is required, and then the various pieces developed to this point must be fit together in an internally consistent fashion. Only the outlines of the full aggregate model are developed here, though, as this will be sufficient to establish the context for the analyses in the following chapters.

The first matter which requires consideration is the relation between the price of services in the markets for rental and owner-occupied housing, i.e., the relation between P_{so} and P_{sr}. From the argument in the previous sections, it is evident that some of the difference between P_{so} and P_{sr} arises from the characteristics of the housing stock. Demand will depend on the composition as well as the level of services available. This is to say that an apartment and a single-family detached dwelling may provide the same quantity of housing services, but their structural difference may make each more or less valuable to given households. In short, they are imperfect substitutes.

An empirical factor of consequence, then, is the extent to which the same housing stock can be employed in either the rental or homeownership market. If demanders from each market must compete for the same units, in general it will be appropriate to include only a single supply function in an aggregate model for housing services but not attempt to consider the two markets in isolation from one another.

In theory any unit could be rented or owned, if the price for either tenure form became great enough. Presumably the market has over time provided dwelling units better suited for each tenure form in response to changes in demand and before the conversion of structures normally rented or owner-occupied have been moved into the other tenure form on a widespread basis. By examining the range of switch-overs, i.e., the number of units "normally" consumed in one tenure form actually consumed in the other form, some idea of the flexibility of the stock and the separability of the markets can be obtained. The evidence in the final section of Chapter 2 provides a fairly clear picture on this point. The stock is quite flexible between tenure forms, but not so flexible that one could view owner-occupants and renters as competing for the same services throughout. Therefore an aggregate model of tenure choice and housing consumption needs to include separate supply functions for housing services under each tenure form and to treat the supply of services in each as simultaneously determined.

In past studies of housing demand no differentiation has been made of the supply functions facing owners and renters or other groups.[10] The previous argument shows that the distinction is an important one for this analysis. One can think of the relation between the price per unit of service at which housing is supplied for each tenure form as being the same at the time at which the services are produced, but that they potentially differ over time due to imperfect matching of housing stock characteristics with the services that are demanded. For expository purposes the relation between the price of services under each tenure at a point in time can be written as

$$P_{so} = P_{sr} + \alpha Z \tag{3.10}$$

where Z is a vector of the characteristics of the stock. In (3.10) the sole source of divergence between P_{so} and P_{sr} stems from the mismatching of the stock with the demand for tenure form, and thus the derived demand for certain structural attributes, with the existing stock. An examination of the stock and service supply functions for owners and the service supply function of renters shows that for this type of mismatch to be the sole cause of price differences would require potentially unrealistic assumptions.[e] However, (3.10) does depict what is seen as a major source of divergence between P_{so} and P_{sr}: structural differences.

These ideas are incorporated into the aggregate model by expressing the supply functions as:

$$P_{so} = n \left(P_k, Q_o^q, P_o, Z, Q \right) \tag{3.11a}$$

$$P_{sr} = n \left(P_c, P_o, Q_r^q, Z, Q \right). \tag{3.11b}$$

The prices are the average prices per unit of capital, operating inputs, etc., as defined previously. Q_o^q and Q_r^q are, respectively, the average quantity of services purchased by owner-occupant and rental households; and Q is the aggregate quantity of services purchased in the market. These functions are similar to those developed in the previous section. Both prices depend on the overall level of demand, on the characteristics of the stock, and on the average quantity of services demanded by an owner or renter. Note that the characteristics of the stock affect demand through the price per unit of services, and P_{sr} and P_{so} are kept from diverging to any great extent by the sensitivity of demand to the relative prices of services under each tenure form.

---

[e]For example, the price of operating and capital inputs must be the same to owner-occupants' and landlords and the level of services demanded by the same under both tenure forms. For a discussion of likely differences in factor prices by tenure, see Appendix A of R. Struyk and L. Ozanne, "Conceptual Analysis of Landlords and Owner-Occupants." Some estimates of the differences in operating *costs* between the two forms of tenure are given by J. Shelton in "The Costs of Renting Versus Owning a Home," *Land Economics*, 1968, pp. 59-72.

The second factor which needs to be included in moving from a model of individual behavior to one of aggregate behavior is race. The racial effects to be included in the demand function are not those which are highly colinear with other variables in the function such as income or family composition. The real consideration is racial segregation and/or discrimination. As discussed more fully in Chapter 6, to the extent that racial segregation exists in an area and is largely coincidental with poor-quality housing, and/or multi-unit structures, the rate of homeownership by the minority will be reduced. The incidence of homeownership for blacks may also be constricted by poor information available from real estate agents, by restrictive financing practices by mortgage companies and by other factors.[11] The differences in owner-occupancy and the related type of dwelling occupied by white and black households can be appreciated from the data in Figures 2-3 and 2-4 for St. Louis which were reviewed in the last chapter. The lower incidence of single-unit structures and homeownership, to the extent it is produced by segregation and discrimination, is the phenomena to be captured by our "race" variable.

The actual formulation of the aggregate model is heavily based on the of owner-occupant and rental services demand and supply (3.7 and 3.8) and the tenure choice decision (3.9); but this model requires more than simply aggregating over the households and introducing the factors just discussed. The model is formally stated in Appendix F, and only a few of its salient features are noted here. The general view embodied in the model is that the supply and consumption decisions in the owner and renter markets are closely related and must, therefore, be treated as being simultaneously determined. On the demand side, four phenomena are determined in the model by behavioral relationships: the aggregate probability of owner-occupancy, the average quantity of housing services per household demanded in the market, the average services demanded by owner-occupant households, and the average housing stock demanded by owner-occupants.[f] The aggregate probability of renting and the average quantity of housing per household demanded by renters are determined through identities. Simultaneously, the interaction of supply and demand determines the price per unit of owner-occupied and rental housing services and of owner-occupant housing stock. The joint determinancy of these phenomena is strongly emphasized.

In line with earlier arguments, the model relates the markets for owner-occupant and rental housing through (a) the endogenous price terms in the demand functions; (b) the total market demand for housing; (c) the supply functions for both owner-occupant and rental housing as P_{sr} and P_{so} depend in part on total demand and the characteristics of the entire housing stock (Z); and (d) through a series of identities. The complexity of the determination of the rate of owner-occupancy and the consumption of housing services in a given market is

---

[f]The model is formulated in terms of the aggregate tenure and consumption decisions of owner-occupant households, although it could have been expressed in terms of renters.

evident from the model just formulated. While its complexity, through stringent data requirements, precludes estimating any model as complete as that expressed in Appendix F, this formulation does provide a broad overall framework and perspective in which to place the partial models formulated and tested in the remainder of the volume.

Part II:
Econometric Estimates

4

Determinants of Tenure Choice in a Single Housing Market

Introduction

As noted in the opening chapter, there are two major reasons for analyzing the determinants of tenure choice within a single housing market. First, because the price of housing services under each tenure form is the same throughout the market[a] and the available housing stock is the same for all households, the primary determinants of tenure choice within the market will be the economic, social, and demographic characteristics of the households. Thus we have the opportunity to study how the characteristics of individual households affect the ownership decision, given market conditions; this is an opportunity which is not available to us in the cross-market studies presented in the next two chapters.

The second reason is that it is only by determining the general form of the income-tenure choice relation using individual household data that the requisite empirical information for modeling the same relation in the aggregate can be obtained. Separating the effect of a household's income from market effects is most efficiently done by restricting the analysis to a single market.

It is quite remarkable that despite the intense economic research on the demand for housing services within urban areas, there has been much less study, theoretical or applied, of the determinants of tenure choice in the same markets. Only the efforts of Maisel, Fredland, Projector and Weiss, Bossons, and Kain and Quigley have focused on the tenure decision; and these in general suffer from three distinct limitations which the present study has attempted to overcome.[1]

None of the previous studies has examined the relationship between income and tenure choice in detail. Maisel examines income as a determinant of tenure through a number of enlightening two-way cross-classifications, describing the role of (current) income at various points in the life cycle and for various ethnic and geographic subgroups in the Los Angeles area. In his statistical work, though, income enters as a linear variable without justification. Kain and Quigley

---

[a]There has recently been considerable discussion and some evidence supporting the hypothesis that prices for standard bundles of housing services may vary within an urban area due to interaction between structural and locational characteristics of the housing units. Throughout this volume, we reject this notion. Empirically it can be argued that the variations being observed by the authors noted below arise from specification errors in their estimates. The strongest proponents of the within market variations are William Apgar and J.F. Kain; see their "Neighborhood Attributes and the Residential Price Geography of Urban Areas," paper presented at the Econometric Society Meetings, December 1972. For a test of their hypothesis see A.B. Schnare and R. Struyk, "Testing for Housing Market Segmentation," *Journal of Urban Economics*, forthcoming.

also settle on a linear form after some experimentation. Fredland, on the other hand, uses a non-linear form but provides little theoretical defense for its use. Additionally, among these earlier studies only Kain and Quigley made any attempt to include a measure of permanent income.[b]

The second limitation of the previous studies has been their aggregation across family types,[c] and in Maisel's case also across housing markets. Fredland divides households into husband-wife households and "others" for his estimates. Maisel, and Kain and Quigley include all households in a single estimated model, differentiating among household types and life cycle position with dummy variables.[d] A central hypothesis, then, that these earlier studies leave largely untested is of differing relationships between income and tenure choice by age and household type.

A third limitation of these studies has been the concentration on the tenure decision of relocating and newly formed households. The basic argument in favor of studying only these households is that it is only when a household moves that it has the opportunity to adjust its housing consumption to an equilibrium position; stationary households with the passage of time move away from this equilibrium. High moving costs especially for owner-occupants prevent frequent moves, which means that moves will only be made in the face of major disequilibria. There are two basic arguments against the position taken in these earlier studies. First, it in general requires an assumption of substantial myopia on the part of relocating households. It seems probable that relocating households make the level-of-services and tenure decisions based at least in part on future housing requirements as well as those of the moment, both in terms of family size and composition and expected income. Thus recently relocated households may be as far from disequilibria as those who lived in a house for twenty years.[e] Second, movers may constitute a subset of the population who

[b]To approximate permanent income the authors replaced observed household income with the mean incomes of the sample households stratified by the race and years of education of the head of household. As the authors note, this should reduce the transitory component of income. No estimates were reported in which both current and permanent income were included in the same regression model.

[c]All of the previous studies combined households of different races. Only Kain-Quigley address the issue of possible differences in determinants of tenure choice by race, and they conclude "As with the ownership models, separate Negro and white equations were estimated for the probability of purchase. Except for their intercepts they were identical and a covariance test indicated no statistically different relationship." (p. 265) Nevertheless, we have estimated separate models for each race to further test the hypothesis of systematic differences.

[d]Kain-Quigley note that they did estimate separate models for three groups of non-husband-wife households, although the models are not included in their published estimates.

[e]One can hypothesize that the direction of the disequilibria will vary systematically over the life cycle of standard families for both recent purchasers and others. In young ages the household buys more housing than currently required in anticipation of family growth; in its middle years it most closely approximates current services and "need"; in old age it holds more than needed either because of inertia or because of a taste for "their own home." At all points in the cycle there is little reason to expect those relocating to behave differently from others.

differ in significant ways from the total population. There will be more renters in a sample of movers than in the total population simply because renters have a higher propensity to move. Further, both renters and owner movers may differ from their subpopulations. It has been shown that certain groups have higher relocation rates than others;[2] those with greater expectations of relocating again in the near future may deliberately choose non-equilibrium positions, either economizing "this time" or "splurging for once." In brief, a large number of arguments can be arrayed for the determinants of the tenure choice of movers to differ quantitatively from that of others, but the argument that these determinant values represent equilibrium seems weak.

The present study is focused primarily on the relationship between tenure choice and income. The functional relationship is of the s-shaped form specified in Figure 3-3 and justified in the accompanying text. Measures of both current and permanent income are used in the empirical analysis. Like the Fredland and Kain-Quigley studies, households from a single housing market, in the present case the Pittsburgh SMSA, are used as the sample.

Households have been disaggregated into six types for each race: four husband-wife household types divided by the age of the head, an "other family" type, and primary individuals. We have attempted to include among the explanatory variables those which measure explicitly the effect of the federal income tax advantages of homeownership on the tenure decision. Certain household characteristics, e.g., family size and composition, have also been taken into account.

The remainder of this chapter consists of five sections. The first presents the theoretical framework. It is followed by a discussion of the specification of the variables and econometric techniques used. The next two sections contain the results of estimating the models for white and black households, respectively. The final section lists some conclusions.

Theoretical Framework

Aside from equity or investment considerations, the determinants of household tenure choice are essentially the same set as those for the demand for housing services. Tenure choice is a single, albeit very important, aspect of housing demand. From past studies of the demand for housing services and the discussion in Chapter 3, one would expect the tenure decision to depend on household type and age, family size, race, and income. This list is augmented later, but for now it offers a convenient starting point for our discussion of tenure choice generally and the relation between tenure choice and income in particular.

The effects which family type, preference for owner-occupancy, and federal income tax advantages of homeownership have on the tenure decision can be examined through use of indifference curve diagrams. (A more thorough treatment of tax advantages plan is given in Appendix B.) A slight variant of the standard diagram is used, which can be described with reference to Figure 4-1a. The diagram generally depicts the consumption possibilities of housing services and all other goods by means of the budget lines which are drawn. The budget lines are for two households, one (household 2) more affluent than the other (household 1).

Although the general relationship is between other goods (X) and housing services (H), use of two horizontal scales permits us to distinguish between owner-occupied and rental services. One horizontal scale measures the units of owner-occupied housing services (Ho); the other scale measures units of rental housing services (Hr). Separate budget lines are shown in Figure 4-1 for owners (O) and renters (R); and each is drawn with reference to its own horizontal scale. That is, the intercept of the owner budget line on the horizontal axis indicates the amount of owner occupied housing services he could purchase if he spent all its income on these services.

The households in Figure 4-1a have no preference for one tenure form over the other, as indicated by both the owner and renter scales representing equivalent quantities of services at each point. For example, points B and B′, respectively, indicate 100 units of rental and owner-occupied housing. The horizontal scales in Figures 4-1b and 4-1c, on the other hand, demonstrate situations in which there is a preference for owner-occupied and a preference for rented housing services, respectively. Points BB′ in Figure 4-1b, for example, indicate that it takes 300 units of rental housing to offer the equivalent satisfaction yielded by 200 units of owner-occupied housing. Thus the relative positions of the budget lines indicate the result of both tenure preference and differences in the price of housing services by type of tenure.

Figure 4-1a shows two budget lines for each household, the budget constraint each would face if it were an owner (O) and that it would face if it were a renter (R). The differences between O and R arise here because of the advantageous treatment of certain home expenses of owner-occupants. The magnitude of these advantages depend both on the level of income (tax rate) and the quantity of services consumed adjusted for the fraction subject to preferential treatment for each household. It is this combination of factors which accounts for O_1 being above R_1 only when a relatively large fraction of income is devoted to housing[3] and for O_1 bending slightly away from the horizontal axis as it approaches it.[4]

Let us return now to the case in which a single, moderate income household has a definite preference for owner-occupied housing. This is the situation depicted in Figure 4-1b. Again only the budget lines are shown. In this instance, though, other factors which effect the relative prices of owner-occupied and rental housing, such as the availability of single unit structures in the overall market, are allowed to enter.

At CC′ the household is indifferent between tenure form; that is it is indifferent between, say, 50 units of rental services and 33 units of owner-occupied services, because at this particular point the portion of its income devoted to housing is the same for both. Simultaneously, of course, its preference for owner-occupied housing is satisfied. The relative positions of the budget line show that the household will maximize its utility by being an owner at all levels of housing consumption beyond CC′. Such preferences for owner-occupied housing are typical of middle-aged husband-wife families, especially those with children.

Preferences for rental housing as typically associated with unrelated individuals and very young families are depicted in Figure 4-1c. In this case the pecuniary advantages of ownership do not offset the preferences for rental tenure until a greater quantity of housing is consumed than was the case in Figure 4-1b, i.e., DD′ is to the right of CC′. In brief the relative positions of the owner and renter budget lines reflect the trading off of pecuniary advantages against household preferences. For some family types (like those in Figure 4-1b) the preferences and pecuniary advantages are in the same direction so that rental tenure dominates ownership over only a small portion of the entire possibility set.

Finally, Figure 4-1d shows the equilibrium consumption of housing services and tenure choice for a single household which has a modest preference for ownership. As drawn, the household chooses to be an owner-occupant. Clearly, though, a counterclockwise rotation of the indifference curve would both switch the tenure choice and reduce the quantity of housing services consumed.

The income concept relevant in the tenure choice decision is normal or permanent income. This is consistent with the argument made at the outset of the chapter with respect to the point in time at which the household is in equilibrium with respect to its consumption of housing services generally. Just as a long-run view of the household's housing needs is adopted for its tenure decision, so too is a long-run view of its expected income. This is the standard argument made with regard to any long-lived good. Consequently, the household's permanent income is the concept which is stressed in this analysis.

An additional factor affecting the household's tenure decision, which has received little previous attention, is the tenure choice of the household's peer group. The hypothesis is that the satisfaction which one household derives from owning its home depends on whether members of its peer group are homeowners. Many examples of such dependence are available. Consider the household headed by a blue-collar worker who would like to live in the same area as his fellow workers. If his fellow workers are homeowners and live where there are few rental units, living near them may require buying a home. Similarly, many employees arriving from other cities have residential areas recommended to them by their fellow workers, which frequently imply one tenure choice. One might further hypothesize that there will be a life cycle pattern to the importance of peer group tenure choice. A young household whose head was not "settled" on an occupation should be less influenced by choices by his fellow

52

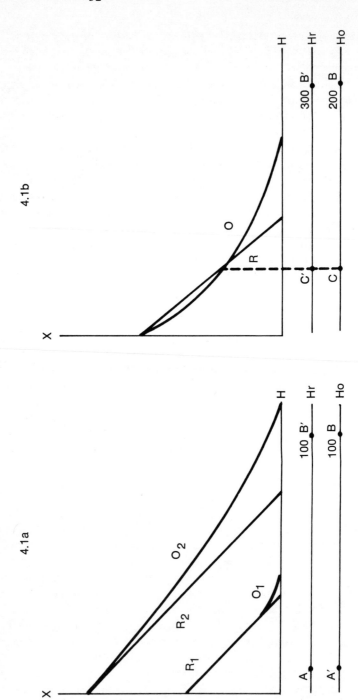

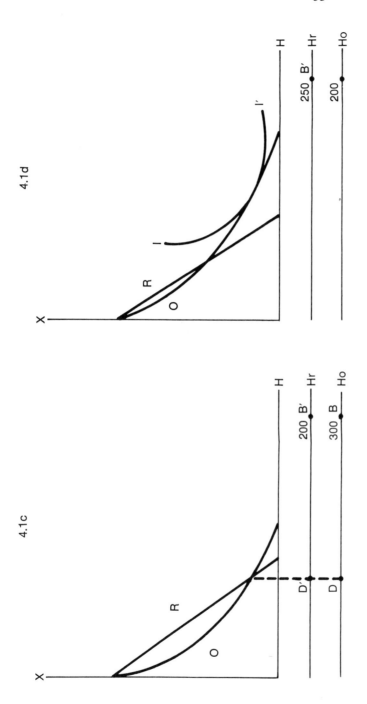

Figure 4-1. Indifference Curve Analysis of Tenure Choice Decision

workers; similarly, aged households exercise steadily decreasing range of choice with economic and health factors likely reducing their ability and desire to emulate the tenure choice of dominantly younger peers. The greatest influence of peer-group tenure choice should be for middle-aged households, in our analysis those in the 30-44 and 45-65 age brackets.

Collecting the above thoughts, a model of tenure choice for a household j of some family type i can be written as:

$$T_{ji} = b_0 + b_1 Y_{ji} - b_2 Y_{ij}^2 + b_3 \text{pers}_{ji} + b_4 \text{fam}_{ji} + b_5 S_j + b_6 \text{peers}_j \qquad (4.1)$$

T_{ji} = the tenure choice of household j of family type i being an owner-occupant, with 1 indicating owner-occupant and zero otherwise.

Y_{ji} = the permanent income of the household, written in this quadratic form to emphasize the declining importance of income at higher income levels in the expected functional relationship.

pers_{ji} = the number of persons in household j of family type i.

fam_{ji} = summarizes other characteristics of household j which may be important, e.g., presence of nonrelatives, aged family member in youthful household, etc.

S_j = the federal income tax subsidy from homeownership available to j; it is the same for all household types.

peer_j = the average probability of homeownership of j's peer group; the same for all household types.

This is the basic model used in the analysis.

A more complete model was also specified and estimated in which the homeownership decision, the expenditures on housing services, and the subsidy from federal income tax advantages of homeownership were jointly or simultaneously determined. The model and estimates of it are presented in Appendix A. The joint determinacy was supported for only three of the six household types for which the model was estimated. An important point in the present context, though, is that even where joint determinacy was supported, the tenure choice-income relation was generally unaffected. This means the estimates of the same relation obtained from applying (4.1) should generally not suffer from a simultaneous equation bias. It also provides some justification for using the very partial model depicted in (4.1) when the complexities of the ownership decision were carefully specified in the previous chapter.

Specification of Variables and Estimation Procedures

The data used in this study are the 1-in-100 1970 Census public use sample for the Allegheny and Westmoreland Counties of the Pittsburgh metropolitan area.[5]

This Census sample is more suited to the study of tenure choice than similar earlier samples because for the first time identification of an individual metropolitan area—and, therefore, a single housing market—has been possible. Additionally the sample size is large enough to permit estimation of separate models for quite narrowly defined household types.

Specification of Variables

Tenure choice. As the choice is discrete it is treated as a binary variable with one indicating owner-occupancy and zero rental occupancy.

Income. The need to use a measure of "normal" or permanent family income instead of the income of the family at some arbitrary point in time in making estimates of the income elasticity of the demand for housing has become well established among economists. The arguments are equally strong with respect to the tenure choice. The Census 1-in-100 user's sample provides information on the family's income in 1969. It was necessary, therefore, as a preliminary step to estimate permanent family income on the basis of observed income and the productive capabilities of the family members.

While the actual estimates of permanent income are described in some detail in Appendix C, the following briefly summarizes the two-step method employed: (1) a multiple regression model was estimated in which total family income was determined by a separate set of independent variables for each household member which measured each member's human capital and labor force participation and (2) values of the same independent variables were substituted into the estimated model to obtain predicted permanent income. In this step, all households were assumed to be in the same age group to abstract from the life-cycle earnings pattern, and each member was assigned the average labor force participation probability of his sex-race group. Note that by using total family income as the dependent variable the effects of wealth holdings to the extent they augment income should be reflected in the predicted permanent income.

In obtaining actual estimates, measures of both permanent and current income have been included for two reasons. First, there are likely to be errors associated with our estimates of permanent incomes for which inclusion of current incomes may account. Second, the transitory component of income may be quite important in determining the timing of the decision to buy a home. For example, one would expect a large positive transitory component for younger husband-wife families to be positively related to owner-occupancy.

Subsidy rates. Three alternative measures of the federal income tax subsidy available to homeowners have been used. These are summarized here and described in greater detail in Appendix B. The first measure makes use of the differences in the federal income tax rates of otherwise similar homeowners and non-homeowners under the 1966 income tax law as computed by Aaron.[f]

The second estimate provides a subsidy rate for each specific household but requires a strong assumption to permit their calculation. As detailed in Appendix B, if one assumes a unitary income elasticity of demand for housing services, then the reduction in federal income taxes as income rises associated with housing deductions is directly related to the fraction of (permanent) income expended on housing. In computing this potential subsidy for renters one is confronted necessarily with making the assumption that housing expenditures would be the same for the household under both tenure forms. For this and other reasons this measure is less satisfactory than the first.[g] The third measure of the tax subsidy is the marginal tax rate on permanent income which the household faces.

Other household characteristics. Initially six family types were specified for both white and black households, but sample size limitations made it necessary to aggregate the four black husband-wife samples into two. The resulting household types and their sample sizes are shown in Table 4-1. The age categories within the husband-wife families were defined so as to be consistent with the categories for which the Census makes available aggregate data. Separate estimates for black and white households are being undertaken because it is believed that the various constraints on the housing choice of blacks implies that essentially separate housing markets may exist for each race. This in turn may significantly affect the observed behavior of households of the two races.

Table 4-1
Sample Sizes by Family Type and Race

Family Type	Sample Size	
	Whites	Blacks
Husband-wife families, head		
Under age 30	327	80
Age 30-44	707	
Age 45-65	1,084	110
Over age 65	193	
Other Families	278	74
Primary Individuals	411	68

[f]Using the Brookings tax file he computed the differences by age of taxpayer (under and over sixty-five) and for those filing returns with itemized and standard deductions.

[g]A central shortcoming of this measure is that the expenditure-income ratio could also reflect the taste of the family for housing and other factors instead of or in addition to tax subsidy benefits.

While estimating models for specific household types greatly reduces the variability among households, considerably greater precision is possible by controlling for other household characteristics. The most important of these is clearly the number and age of children present; two variables are used to account for this, the number of children under six years of age and the number between six and eighteen. Another factor which might strongly influence the tenure decision is the presence of an elderly person in the household. To account for this the number of persons over age sixty, excluding the head, is included as a variable. The presence of boarders or nonrelatives in the household may also be important, consequently dummy variables for the presence of each of these is included. Finally, five age-class, dummy variables are included in the models for the households of the "other family" and "primary individual" type.

Tenure choice of peer group. Two specifications of peer groups were initially adopted based on the occupations and education of household heads. The fraction of households who were owner-occupants and the average housing expenditures were calculated for each of the ten occupation and eight education classes. The values of these variables along with the average consumption of peer-group housing consumption expenditures are displayed in Table 4-2.

Each household in the micro-samples has its average peer-group values assigned to it; no distinction by age or family type is made. Given the large number of observations in most cells, and the very broad definition of peer group, it is doubtful that any real identification problem exists. Our general view was that the occupational groupings were more effective, and these generally performed more satisfactorily in the estimated models.

Much of this discussion is summarized in Tables 4-3 and 4-4, which present the mean values of a number of characteristics of the included households by household type for whites and blacks respectively.

Estimation Procedures

As is well known use of a binary dependent variable limits the resulting estimates in two ways: (1) the standard errors of the coefficients of the estimated model may be biased owing to heteroskedasticity; and (2) the values of the dependent variable predicted using the estimated model may fall outside of the interval 0 to 1.[6] The main purpose of the present analysis is to test hypotheses concerning the tenure decision, not to classify households into the two tenure classes. Therefore, the second limitation does not strongly affect the present estimates; but the first clearly does.

Given a model with a binary dependent variable, estimation can be accomplished through several procedures including disriminant analysis and generalized linear regression. Assuming that either of these two will provide

Table 4-2
Peer Group Tenure Choice and Housing Expenditures

Peer Groups	Renters Gross Rent	Owners Value of House	Fract. Owner- Occupants	No. of Households
A. Occupation				
Professional, managers	$159.6	$26,097	.753	841
Sales	137.6	20,624	.698	225
Clerical	115.8	13,342	.579	373
Craftsmen	99.6	14,387	.774	655
Operatives, pt. transport.	90.3	13,138	.653	340
Transport operatives	101.6	13,202	.642	154
Laborers	95.0	12,121	.586	133
Farmers or farm workers	–	30,000	1.0	2
Service workers	91.3	12,378	.120	303
Domestics	83.0	7,800	.672	8
B. Education–years of school				
None	$135.4	$11,520	.706	17
Some grade school	75.7	12,730	.769	65
Grade school graduate	76.7	9,839	.609	64
Some high school	89.0	12,750	.720	535
High school graduate	93.7	14,236	.614	272
Some college	114.0	15,600	.691	1,372
College graduate	127.8	21,220	.692	133
Post-graduate work	165.8	30,040	.681	577

unbiased estimates of the coefficients and of the statistics of the quality of the estimated model, the choice between them depends mainly on the process underlying the two.[7] Whereas regression analysis seeks to minimize the unexplained variance in the dependent variable, discriminant analysis maximizes the distance between the two groups relative to the intra-group values of the same variables. Discriminant analysis has the added feature that as a matter of course it forces the relation between the dependent (or discriminated) variable and the independent variables to be similar to that shown in Figure 3-3. This a priori justifiable form is one which cannot be duplicated in regression analysis when the dependent variable is binary.

Ultimately two empirical observations argued for use of regression analysis. First, comparisons of identical regression models estimated using ordinary

(OLS) and generalized (GLS)[h] least squares indicated that while use of GLS greatly increased the degree of explained variance in the dependent variable, the coefficients of the independent variables did not change significantly. Therefore, no overriding concern with this problem seemed to be required, although GLS has often been used in reestimating final forms. The second observation is based on estimates of the tenure choice model shown in (4.1) in which permanent income entered as a series of dummy variables for income intervals. That is, each $2,000 interval, except the lowest, was represented by a different zero/one independent variable—one when the household's permanent income fell in that interval and zero otherwise. The pattern of the relation shown by the coefficients of these variables was shown to be definitely non-linear but not clearly s-shaped; thus use of discriminant analysis which forces this functional form seemed questionable. The functional relations found to best represent the underlying relationship are presented in the next section.

Results for White Households

The results are organized into three sections which correspond to our special interest in some aspects of the findings. The first section presents data on the relationship between income and tenure choice. The second discusses the peer group tenure choice variable in the models for various family types. The final section gives the estimates of the effects of federal tax subsidies, as we have measured them, on the tenure decision.

Tenure Choice and Income

The starting point for our empirical exploration of this relationship was to examine the coefficients of a group of permanent income dummy variables to ascertain the general shape of the relation. Based on this we tried various transformations of the continuous permanent variable to approximate the

[h]The GLS estimates were made by weighting all variables of each observation by:

$$\left[\frac{1}{P(1-P)} \right]^{1/2}$$

where P is the calculated probability derived from an OLS estimate. This procedure is recommended by Goldberger, *Econometric Theory* (New York: John Wiley and Sons, 1965). It is shown to give consistent estimates by R.G. McGillivray in "Estimating the Linear Probability Function," *Econometrica* 38 (1970).

Table 4-3
Mean Values of Selected Variables for White Households

	Husband-Wife Families with Male Heads				Other Family	Primary Individual
	Under Age 30	Age 30-44	Age 45-65	Over Age 65		
Income						
Current income	10,249	12,448	14,348	10,111	9,104	6,101
Permanent income	14,040	12,899	11,268	9,474	6,212	6,839
Household composition						
Children under age 6	.954	.655	.067	.026	.129	–
Children under age 18	1.144	2.47	.878	.067	.784	–
Members over 65, incl. head	.006	.051	.165	.927	.360	.022
Boarders present, 1 = yes	.006	.003	.006	–	.028	.043
Nonrelatives present, 1 = yes	.006	.001	.001	–	.004	.051
Nonwife or child relatives present, 1 = yes	.037	.072	.107	.072	.514	–
Number of persons in household	3.18	4.66	3.44	2.37	2.87	1.12
Distribution of no. of persons						
2	.306	.085	.351	.767	.558	.077
3-4	.596	.390	.440	.187	.327	.015
5-6	.088	.413	.165	.041	.097	.002
Fraction female headed					.705	.594

Age distribution of head					
under 24				.032	.294
24-44				.219	.355
45-54				.309	.151
55-65				.277	.141
over 65				.162	.058
Housing consumption					
Fraction owner-occupied	.385	.795	.847	.762	.590	.350
Fraction occupation peer-group owner-occupants	.705	.711	.702	.705	.653	.663
Fraction education peer-group owner-occupants	.684	.684	.687	.694	.689	.689
Ownership subsidy measures					
"Aaron subsidy"	2.06	1.99	1.93	1.89	1.13	1.41
"Calculated subsidy"	.090	.133	.126	.199	.193	.190
Permanent income tax rate	.217	.204	.200	.193	.193	.223
Number of households in sample	327	707	1,084	193	288	111

Table 4-4
Mean Values of Selected Variables for Black Households

	Husband-Wife Families With Head			
	Under Age 44	Over Age 44	Other Family	Primary Individual
Income				
Current income	8,219	8,000	4,939	3,560
Permanent income	7,440	6,724	4,138	4,755
Household composition				
Children under age 6	.775	.082	.500	–
Children under age 18	2.19	.982	1.64	–
Members over 65, excl. head	.025	.373	.122	.015
Boarders present, 1 = yes	.012	.027	.027	.029
Nonrelatives present, 1 = yes	.012	.009	.013	.029
Nonwife, nonchild relatives present, 1 = yes	.075	.182	.324	–
Numbers of persons in household	4.65	3.58	3.32	1.12
Distribution of number of persons				
2	.112	.418	.365	.029
3-4	.487	.300	.473	.015
5-6	.212	.209	.135	.015
Fraction nonhusband-wife households:				
Female headed			.784	.500
Head under 24 years old			.108	.073
Head 24-44			.500	.265
Head 45-54			.189	.265
Head 55-65			.108	.235
Over 65			.094	.162
Housing consumption				
Fraction owner-occupied	.400	.645	.257	.191
Fraction occupation peer-group owner-occupants	.656	.636	.643	.646
Ownership subsidy increases				
"Aaron subsidy"	2.15	2.08	1.46	1.13
"Calculated subsidy"	.121	.139	.193	.161
Permanent income tax rate	.171	.170	.169	.194
Number of households in sample	80	110	74	68

indicated relationship. Two factors complicated this simple procedure. For some family types the regression coefficients for the group of permanent income (PY) dummy variables were not significantly different from zero. Second, for reasons already outlined, it was desirable to include current income (CY) in the model as well as PY; and the interaction between the two needed to be determined. To obtain what was thought to be the "best" relation extensive experimentation was undertaken with functional forms which approximated the basic relationship.

Figure 4-2 contains a graph of the probability of homeownership-income relations for each of the six family types based on the OLS regression models presented in Table 4-5.[i] The graphs were drawn to demonstrate the functional relationship in question. The effects of other variables are held fixed at their mean values. "Income" refers to both CY and PY and the graph shows their combined effect. Permanent income at a given level of CY was determined from the relation between PY and CY estimated for each family type.

As noted at the end of the previous section, the estimated models using the group of dummy variables for permanent income intervals did not demonstrate the underlying s-shaped relation which had been anticipated. This is reflected in the graphs in Figure 4-2. The deviation from the expected functional form is an important point and one which requires comment.

Several explanations seem possible. The first, and most convincing, is that the relatively flat portion of the curve for low incomes is very small and therefore difficult to discern empirically. A second reason may be that our data are not

---

[i]As noted earlier in these models we have purposely omitted the household expenditures, E, from the list of independent variables on the basis of the results for the simultaneous equation models. Nevertheless, if one considers E to be strictly exogenous and to be dominantly a function of income, Y, i.e., $E = \alpha Y$, then the income elasticities as presented here are upward biased. Let tenure choice be determined by

$$T = b_0 + b_1 X + b_2 Y + b_3 E.$$

Then the coefficient of income which we have estimated will be $b_2 + b_3 \alpha$ and the true elasticity is overstated by $b_3 \alpha\ Y_i/T_i$. In practice E and Y are closely related, as documented in many housing demand studies, so that including both in the model at hand produces high multicollinearity and biased estimates. One way to bracket the degree of "overlap" is to estimate separate models for T including only E or Y among the independent variables and to examine the confidence intervals around the coefficients. This has not been done here because of the number and complexity of the income variables in most functions.

A second point concerns our treatment of the peer group tenure variable as strictly exogenous. If the reader feels this is not the case, our arguments of the previous section notwithstanding, the proper adjustment to income elasticities would be to multiply them by $\dfrac{1}{1-b}$ where b is the coefficient of the peer group coefficient, for the husband-wife age 30-44 and 45-65 models in which this variable is significant. In the first instance this adjustment will roughly double the elasticities while in the second it increases them by a factor of 2.5.

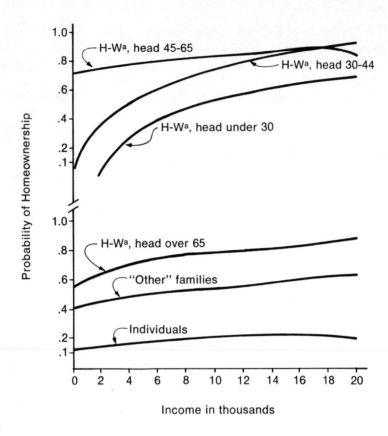

aHusband-wife families.

Figure 4-2. Relation Between Probability of Homeownership and Income

accurate enough to determine the point of inflection. Third it is possible that there are a sufficient number of low (permanent and current) income households who purchased their homes during particularly prosperous times in the past which neither of the income measures reflect. This results in the expected relation between ownership and incomes at the lower end of the curve being badly clouded. If one could eliminate these "special cases" the full curve might be found. On balance, it does not seem justified to reject the s-shaped relation as the basic functional form on the basis of these findings.

The graphs clearly indicate that for all the family types, except "other," the effect of increments of income increase the probability of homeownership at a decreasing rate. For primary individuals, in fact, an actual decrease was found in the probability at the highest levels of permanent income (see reported regression model). It is evident that the younger husband-wife family types (under age forty-five) are much more responsive to increments of income than other household types. The variation in responsiveness is indicated more accurately by the income elasticities of demand for owner-occupied housing presented in Table 4-6. The five-point elasticities exhibit three distinct patterns. For younger husband-wife families the elasticities are extremely high at low levels of income and steadily decline at higher income levels. For the two older husband-wife family types and primary individuals the elasticities increase and then decrease as income rises; for primary individuals the elasticity actually becomes negative at the highest income levels. The income elasticity for non-husband-wife families increases over the entire income range.

The great diversity in the elasticities among household types provides a reason for some difference between these results and those from other studies of tenure choice which aggregate across households and attempt to account for differences among them with additive dummy variables. One example are the differences in the elasticities obtained here compared with those estimated by Fredland, who aggregated observations into two groups, all husband-wife households and other households.[j] These results additionally indicate the biases probable from specifying income as linear.

Having the overall income-tenure choice relationship in mind, the estimated models upon which the discussion to this point has been based can now be examined with an eye to two specific issues: (1) the comparative strength of CY and PY in the model for each household type, and (2) the other significant determinants of tenure choice. With regard to the first issue, only for the husband-wife over age sixty-five family type were not forms of both PY and CY significant as determinants of tenure choice. For this type only current income was significant, perhaps indicating large errors in the measurement of their permanent income.[k] While both CY and PY are in the other five models, they differ in the combinations of forms in which they occur. For the husband-wife age 45-65 and primary individual household types, no general functional relation for the effect of PY was determined; instead dummy variables for only part of the range of PY were included. For the remaining three household types both PY and CY enter in nonlinear forms although the exact specifications differ. In the models for the younger two husband-wife types, the effects of PY are quantitatively of much greater importance, while in the model for "other

[j]Based on data in Fredland's thesis, we estimate the mean (current) income elasticities for his two groups to be .317 and .825. Fredland also found the nonlinear specification superior, but it is extremely difficult to compare these to ours as they are based only on relocating households and his inclusion only of current income.

[k]One might argue that tenure status prior to retirement is of dominant importance and lack of this variable significantly limits the results. However, to the extent that pre-retirement tenure depended upon pre-retirement income this should be accounted for by the permanent income variable. Thus our emphasis on a possible measurement error.

Table 4-5
Regression Models of Tenure Choice by Family Type for White Pittsburgh Households (Dependent Variable: 1 = Owner-Occupant)

	Husband-Wife Families, Head Age				Other Family	Primary Individual
	Under 30	30-44	45-65	Over 65		
Constant	-1.40 (3.92)	-.607 (3.35)	.066 (.05)	.628 (2.89)	-.213 (.88)	-.089 (1.43)
3-4 persons, 1 = yes		.322 (6.05)				
5-6 persons, 1 = yes		.351 (6.61)				
7+ persons, 1 = yes		.386 (6.03)				
Number of persons			.094 (3.10)		.211 (1.99)	
(Number of persons)^2			-.008 (2.47)		-.024 (1.82)	
ln number of persons	.412 (4.96)					
Current income (00's)		.0024 (3.87)	.0015 (3.54)	.0020 (2.24)	.0011 (2.03)	.0013 (1.48)
(Current income)^2 (00's)		$-4.*10^{-6}$ (2.86)	$-2.1*10^{-6}$ (2.42)	$-3.9*10^{-6}$ (1.94)		$-4.2*10^{-6}$ (1.56)
ln current income	.115 (2.75)					
Permanent income (00's)	.0083 (2.49)	.0075 (4.79)				
(Permanent income)^2 (00's)	$-2.0*10^{-5}$ (2.24)	-.00002 (4.53)				

	(1)	(2)	(3)	(4)	(5)	(6)
(Reciprocal of permanent income) × 100 (00's)					.00042 (1.52)	
Permanent income 12-16 (000), 1 = yes						−.108 (4.83)
16-20 (000), 1 = yes						−.122 (5.68)
Permanent income 4-8 (000), 1 = yes			.094 (3.06)			
8-12 (000), 1 = yes			.069 (2.58)			
Subsidy measure	1.86 (3.89)	.208 (3.16)			.020 (.98)	
Tenure status of occupational peers	.019 (.05)	.460 (2.04)	.601 (3.77)			
Female head, 1 = yes					−.180 (2.65)	
Head: age 24-44, 1 = yes					.283 (1.71)	
age 45-54, 1 = yes					.405 (2.48)	.345 (1.20)
age 55-65, 1 = yes					.589 (3.54)	.346 (5.68)
age 65+, 1 = yes					.456 (2.67)	.301 (1.73)
Aged family member except head, 1 = yes			.051 (1.90)			
R^2	.151	.148	.052	.010	.118	.116
F	10.9	14.8	8.58	2.65	4.80	7.90

Note: Reported models have not been weighted to take account of heteroskedasticity; weighted estimates increase explained variance dramatically. See text for discussion.

Table 4-6

Elasticities of Tenure Choice with Respect to Income for White Household Types at Selected Income Points[a]

Family Type	Income[b]				
	$4,000	$8,000	$12,000	$16,000	$20,000
Husband-Wife Families					
1. Head under age 30	1.90	1.19	.786	.555	.424
2. Head age 30-44	.847	.700	.576	.464	.331
3. Head age 45-65	.170	.183	.211	.222	.163
4. Head age 65	.112	.141	.154	.136	.091
Other Families	.091	.168	.232	.268	.335
Primary Individual	.239	.269	.189	.014	−.276

[a]Elasticities are total elasticities of all income terms.

[b]Income shown in column heads is current income. The permanent income corresponding to the current income for each family type was calculated separately and used for permanent income variables.

families" the reciprocal form of *PY* is only marginally significant and of negligible quantitative importance.

In examining the non-income determinants discussion of the peer group and tax subsidy variables is withheld until later sections. With a single exception the only other significant determinant in the husband-wife models was some form of the number of persons in the household. Whether those people were children, boarders, nonrelatives, etc., had no discernible effect on tenure choice. The exception is that the presence of an aged family member in a family with a nonaged head increased the probability of homeownership for husband-wife families aged 45-65 by 5 percent. Again, the form of the relationship between the number of persons and tenure varied markedly across household types. Lastly, in non-husband-wife household types several "standardizing" variables—age and sex of head—are significant determinants.

Tenure Choice of Peer Group

In deciding whether to buy or rent its dwelling unit a household is influenced in two distinct ways by its occupational status. First, there is a difference in average incomes between occupations; and as demonstrated, income is a significant determinant of tenure choice. Second, occupation influences the decision through peer-group pressures as outlined earlier. In including a peer-group variable in the regression model, an attempt is being made to separate this second, more subtle effect of occupational status. If a separate peer-group effect is found, one implication will be that other studies of tenure choice may have overstated the direct effect of income on tenure choice.

As hypothesized above, the tenure choice of the household head's peer group is strongest for the middle-aged husband-wife family types. Based on the coefficients of the peer group variables in Table 4-5, the elasticity of tenure choice with respect to occupational peer group choice evaluated at the means for those household types are:

Husband-wife, head age 40-44: 0.411
Husband-wife, head age 45-65: 0.498

Thus a 10 percent differential among occupation in groups in homeownership rates will change the probability of a household by 0.05, a substantial change.[1]

The Effect of Federal Tax
Subsidies on Tenure

Once again the discussion is based on the estimated models shown in Table 4-5. Of the three measures of the federal tax subsidy employed, only the ratio of housing expenditures to permanent income was found to be of use. The other two, the differential in tax rates between homeowners and others due to housing related deductions computed by Aaron and the marginal tax rate on permanent income, were never significant, seemingly owing to their high correlations with income.[m] In the following discussion only the second measure will be referred to, and it will simply be termed the calculated subsidy or subsidy.

---

[1] A comparison of the models for each two household types with similar models excluding the peer group variables failed to reveal any significant differences in the coefficients of the income terms. So at least in the case at hand the income terms were not biased by the exclusion of a peer group tenure variable.

An interesting question is why peer group tenure choice was not significant in the models for other household types. Two explanations seem plausible. First, the two effects of occupation on tenure choice may become indistinguishable; that is, high status occupation groups have high incomes and high owner-occupancy rates so that the correlation between income and peer group tenure rates becomes high. Second, for some groups it may simply make little difference what one's occupational peer group does. Presumably this situation is most acute for non-husband-wife families. Examination of the simple correlation coefficients between peer group tenure on the one hand and household income and tenure choice on the other generally supports these suppositions.

[m] The simple correlation coefficients between permanent income and these measures are as follows:

Family Type	Aaron Subsidy	Calculated Tax Rate
Husband-wife family		
under age 30	.672	.974
age 30-44	.583	.954
age 45-65	.389	.957
over age 65	.603	.980
Other family	.583	.953
Primary individuals	.564	.981

The calculated subsidy was significant as a determinant of tenure choice for the younger two husband-wife household types. This result is consistent with the findings on the elasticity of tenure choice with respect to income by family type, which showed the same two family types to be by far the most sensitive to incremental income. Households whose tenure choice is highly income elastic should likewise be sensitive to changes in the price of housing which directly alters their real incomes. There is a substantial difference, though, in the elasticity of tenure choice with respect to the subsidy (evaluated at the mean) between the two family types, 0.470 versus 0.038 for the families with heads under thirty and between thirty and forty-four, respectively.

While one can accept the lack of significance of subsidies for other husband-wife families with low tenure income elasticities, it is more difficult for primary individuals. Both their low income elasticity and the lack of responsiveness to their higher tax rates at each income level compared to those filing joint returns is, at first blush, surprising. Recall, however, their low average incomes (current income: $6,100; permanent income: $6,800) which means a relatively small average benefit from the tax subsidy. The group is also quite heterogeneous; and even dividing the sample and estimating two separate models for each group stratified by age, using forty-five as the cut off, did not further strengthen or clarify relationships.

A compelling explanation for the general lack of significance of the subsidy terms is that the subsidy effects are being captured by the income terms. The high correlation between income and the first and third subsidy measures have already been noted. The correlations reflect that the value of the tax provisions on imputed income and mortgage interest payments and property taxes vary with income; likewise the capital gains treatment on the sale of a house and the related provision for carrying over the basis to a new house are more valuable when income is higher. An additional point in this regard is the household's perception of the form of the subsidy. Since the actual subsidy is received annually as a tax rebate for most households, viewing it as windfall income instead of conceiving it as a price adjustment to the monthly mortgage payment seems quite plausible. Combined, these points indicate reinterpreting the income elasticities recorded above as giving the effect on the ownership decision of income both directly and indirectly through the incremental tax benefits provided.[8]

Results for Black Households

This section does not parallel the previous on white households because the results of estimating tenure choice models for black household types differ rather dramatically from those for whites. In particular, it was very difficult to establish statistically significant relationships between tenure choice and the independent variables included in this study. Accordingly this section is composed of two subsections. The first presents the meaningful results which were obtained and outlines those which were less significant statistically; the second offers some further explanations for what has been found.

The Basic Results

As noted in the section on Specification of Variables, black households were grouped into four household types for these estimates. Statistically significant relationships were established for only younger husband-wife families and non-husband-wife families, and even for these the number of phenomena to which tenure choice was significantly related was quite limited.

It is difficult to rationalize why only these two family types exhibited some of the anticipated relations with other variables. However, it is evident from the outset that white and black households in Pittsburgh differ sharply in the determinants of tenure choice.[9]

The results obtained for the two households which were successfully modeled differed somewhat in form from their white counterparts. These differences are in the income and number of persons in the household variables. In the models for black households permanent income was of negligible importance, and the number of persons in the household entered strongly only as an interaction variable with current income. The lack of significance of permanent income may stem in part from the relatively low variation in permanent income within household types compared to both the current income of black households and the current and permanent income of corresponding white households. (See Appendix C for further discussion.) Given that the estimated permanent incomes of black households within a household type are about the same, "current income" may be reflecting measurement errors more than transitory components. For both the household types for which meaningful results were obtained, some form of permanent income entered the model with the expected sign but was only of very marginal significance.

The use of the number of persons-current income interaction variables show these two factors to affect the tenure decision in a multiplicative, i.e., non-additive, manner.[n] The marginal probability of purchasing a home associated with income depends jointly on the level of income and the number of persons in the household. This point is perhaps best made by the graphs in Figure 4-3 which show the slope of income-ownership probability curve changing with the number of persons in the households. The regression models upon which the graphs are based are in Table 4-7. In the models for both household types the number of

---

[n]The interaction variable was not as effective in the models estimated for white households as other specifications, although it was generally significant. For these black household types, by contrast, the interaction form dominated the results for the income terms.

A. Husband-Wife Households, Head Under Age 45

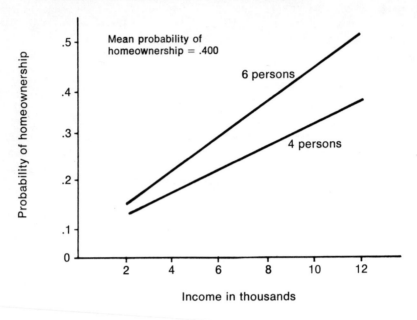

B. Other Family

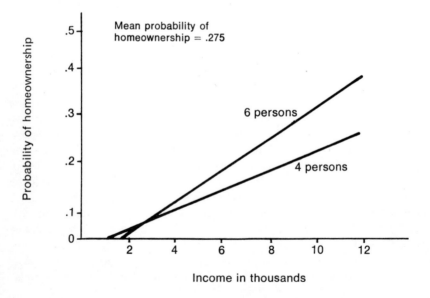

Figure 4-3. Relation Between Income and Tenure Choice

persons in the household has a separate, negative effect on the probability of ownership.[o] This likely indicates the increased difficulty of assembling the necessary downpayment as family size increases.

Table 4-7
Regression Models for Selected Black Household Types

	Husband-Wife, Head Under Age 45		Non-Husband-Wife Families	
	(1)*	(2)	(3)*	(4)
Constant	.512 (4.00)	−1.72 (1.21)	.165 (1.24)	−.498 (1.02)
Persons-income interaction	.0006 (2.44)	.0006 (2.05)	.0007 (2.54)	.0007 (2.33)
No. persons in household	−.053 (1.72)	−.038 (1.16)	−.039 (.10)	.019 (.05)
Head under age 30	−.417 (3.61)	−.431 (3.53)		
Permanent income		.059 (1.58)		
Permanent income^2		−.0004 (1.56)		
Children present, 1 = yes			−.263 (2.43)	−.276 (2.69)
Head age 54-65			.195 (1.70)	.185 (1.60)
Head over age 65			.345 (2.04)	.323 (1.92)
Permanent income, 5,000-6,000				.263 (1.34)
Peer group tenure choice				1.00 (1.35)
Female head			.111 (.98)	.142 (1.25)
$\bar{R}^2$	.171	.177	.294	.318
F	6.85	4.64	7.37	6.07

*Preferred estimate.

---

[o]The appropriate test of statistical significance for interaction variables is not the t-statistics of the individual coefficients but the test of whether the coefficients of all the regressors involving the variable are jointly zero. An F-test of the incremental variance explained by the number of persons and persons-income variable indicates the person variable to be significant in the models shown in Table 4-7. (See Goldberger, *Econometric Theory*, p. 217.) It should be noted, though, that in models excluding income, the persons variable was insignificant. On balance, our view is that person variable itself has little independent influence on the tenure decision. This is supported to a degree by the high significance for the presence-of-children dummy variable in the model for the other household types. In the white household models of children were in no case found to exert a significant influence after the (significant) effect of the number of persons was included in the model. Consequently the discussion in the text focuses on the effect of household size effecting tenure jointly with income.

The marginal effect which certain income-family size combinations have on the probability of ownership are given under A, in Table 4-8. Also shown are the point elasticities of ownership with respect to income for four-person household for both family types. The multiplicative nature of the number of persons and income on the probability of ownership can be appreciated from data in A. Other things being equal, the probability of a young husband-wife household with current annual income of $8,000 will be 0.192 greater for a family of six persons than a family of two, operating jointly with income. The income elasticity for black households under age forty-five is much lower than those for similar white households, while the opposite holds for the "other family" type.

One other significant result requiring comment is the large negative effect which the presence of children in non-husband-wife families has on the probability of homeownership. A family with only the husband or wife present with children under eighteen home has a lower probability (0.26) of being an owner-occupant than similar. families without children. This effect is in addition to the direct and indirect effects of household size (see fn. o). Our suspicion is that this negative effect is acting as a classifying variable in discriminating a

Table 4-8
Data on Effect of Income on Homeownership for Black Household Types

A. Marginal Effects of Income on Probability of Homeownership

	Income			
	$4,000	6,000	8,000	10,000
Husband-Wife, Head Under Age 45				
2 persons	.048	.072	.096	.120
4 persons	.096	.144	.192	.240
6 persons	.144	.216	.288	.360
Non-Husband-Wife Families				
2 persons	.056	.084	.112	.140
4 persons	.112	.168	.224	.280
6 persons	.168	.252	.336	.420

B. Point Income Elasticities for Four-Person Households

	Income			
	$4,000	6,000	8,000	10,000
Husband-Wife, Head Under Age 45[a]	.126	.151	.167	.179
Non-Husband-Wife Families[b]	.636	.420	.359	.330

[a]Based on under age 30 household.

[b]Based on household with children, and head between ages of 54-65.

family with children from other families in this type and as such is accounting for a range of phenomena in addition to the presence of children which result in lower average ownership rates. These households, especially when headed by a female, face more demanding income tests in obtaining mortgages. (See Chapter 6 for further discussion.)

Neither the occupational peer group tenure choice variable or the various measures of the benefits of ownership from federal income tax advantages were significant in these models, although both generally exhibited the expected sign and frequently the coefficients were as large as their standard errors. Neither result is surprising. The occupational peer group variable was computed using average probabilities of homeownership for white households because of the few observations for black households. Average white owner-occupancy probabilties are determined by the incomes, family structures, and other characteristics of white households and whites' putatively greater freedom of choice in the housing markets. Nevertheless, to the extent that black households have occupations which give them rough economic parity with their white occupational peers, some indirect, positive influence on black tenure choice was anticipated. Clearly, though, this influence might be less between races than within.

Below are shown the average current annual incomes and number of persons in the two household types for which significant results were obtained:

	Current Income	Persons/household
Husband-wife, head under age 45	$8,212	4.65
Non-husband-wife families	$4,939	3.32

Evidently for many of these households the benefits derived from itemizing federal income tax deductions when a homeowner would be negligible, given their fairly large personal exemptions. For this reason the lack of significance of the tax subsidy variables was anticipated.[p]

Further Discussion

The reasons for two general aspects of the findings for black households still

---

[p]The more complete models of the joint determination of tenure choice, housing expenditures, and tax subsidies were not estimated for black households as the results of including expenditures in the tenure function and tenure choice in the expenditure function were insignificant and/or not of the expected sign. It might be noted that we were able to obtain significant relations between income and expenditures for all four black household types, so that the lack of significance in the tenure functions appear to be caused by problems in fitting that function and not from a complete randomness in housing demand in terms of income and other phenomena.

need to be examined: (a) why were statistically significant relations established for some household types but not for others; and (b) what accounts for the generally less robust nature of the statistical results for black households compared to white. These two issues are examined in turn below.

Satisfactory statistical relationships were not established for husband-wife families with heads over forty-four (termed elderly families in the following discussion) and primary individuals. With respect to the latter, recall that in some instances there was difficulty obtaining useful estimates for white individuals for which a substantially larger sample was available (411 vs. 68). Likely the combination of small sample size and extreme within group heterogeneity account for our lack of success with black primary individuals. The results for elderly families are less easily explained. The real question is why the regression models were able to successfully discriminate between owner and renters for younger households but not for elderly. The cause does not appear to lie in greater within-group variance for key variables for non-elderly households.[q] Examination of other possible causes gave equally barren results, and little further can be said on the basis of the available data.

The second general aspect of the results for black households to be examined is their overall lower degree of robustness compared to those for white households. The small sample sizes for black households and other reasons for the lack of significance of specific variables have already been noted. Still, other factors may be important in causing the differences in the results. In the next paragraphs an argument for the seeming greater ambivalence of black households concerning tenure choice is set out and, to some extent, supported. Note this is not an argument concerning the lower rates of ownership of black households, but rather it concerns reasons for our inability to distinguish as clearly among black owners and renters as among whites.[r]

Consider that there are three groups of black households in the housing market: owners, renters, and potential owners. Potential owners are households who if confronted by the same housing market conditions as whites would be owners. In essence, many black owners and potential owners are similar except

[q]The coefficients of variation of four independent variables are:

| | Coefficient of variation | |
Variable	Non-elderly	Elderly
current income	45.4	54.0
permanent income	22.6	24.4
no. of children	77.6	154.7
no. of persons	49.0	50.0

[r]The task of explaining differences in average tenure by race really involves an examination across housing markets. The main analysis of this problem to date was done by Kain and Quigley, "Housing Market Discrimination." Also see Chapter 6 of this volume.

for their preference for owner-occupancy. The ambivalence of this group is caused by the unattractive owner-occupancy alternatives *relative* to rental alternatives in the segment of the housing market open to them. The statistical analysis is unable to differentiate among owners and renters in this group because of their similarity in terms of income, family size, and so forth; thus the strength of the regression results is reduced.

To sustain this argument it is necessary to demonstrate: (a) that substantial housing market segregation exists in Pittsburgh; (b) that the ownership alternatives are relatively unattractive relative to rental; (c) that there is a significant group of renters with characteristics similar to those of owners. The following discussion focuses on the first two factors as some similarities between black owners and renters have already been noted.

A simple measure of the extent of residential racial segregation is available in the index developed by Taeuber and Taeuber. The index, which ranges between 0 and 100, is interpreted as "showing the minimum percentage of non-whites who would have to change the block on which they live in order to produce an unsegregated distribution." For the city of Pittsburgh the index had a value of about 85 in both 1960 and 1970. A study of Pittsburgh in earlier years reveals this to be the continuance of long-established pattern of strong racial segregation.[10] In brief, the range of locational choice of black households appears to be restricted.

Documenting the relative attractiveness of owner-occupied versus rental housing is more difficult; however, some suggestive data can be mustered. First, of the single family structures owned and occupied by blacks in 1970, 75 percent were built before 1940 as compared to 46 percent for whites. Purchasing even those older homes in good condition with the expectation that they will deliver the same level services for the life of the mortgage requires a difficult assumption. This compounded with the possibility that they are in neighborhoods with poor public services and possibly above average rates of deterioration and crime makes ownership of these units quite unattractive as an investment. Further, a large portion of the black households will not derive any tax advantage from owner-occupancy. Now, obviously, upper-middle income blacks will not be so constrained; but these are not the ambivalent households.

The counter-argument to the one just presented is that the lower value of the total bundle of services—i.e., short stream of expected services, poor neighborhood conditions, etc.—should be appropriately reflected in a lower sales price and thus if anything encourage home purchase by households with moderate incomes. Two related reasons for black households not purchasing available units even at "objectively" discounted prices seem feasible: (1) fear of deterioration (or further deterioration) in neighborhood quality may make the subjective discount rate higher than the objective; and, (2) households of moderate means typically purchase a home with the intention of living in it for a number of years; thus purchase of a housing stock with only a few years' services remaining is unattractive even if appropriately discounted.[11]

An additional reason for low ownership rates may, though, be the higher price of owner-occupied than rental property to blacks. Such a price differential could easily stem from various restrictive practices on the part of mortgage bankers, insurance companies, and at least until recently, the FHA. The higher price would, of course, eliminate part of the benefits to black ownership. To the extent such restrictive practices exist in Pittsburgh black homeownership has been reduced.[12]

A final factor of probable importance is the relatively large number of single unit structures available for black households to rent. At every income level the proportion of renting black households in such units is greater than the similar proportion for renting white households.[s] About 36 percent of all black renter households are in single-unit structures; Pittsburgh is unusual in this regard among SMSAs in the Northeastern Census Division where the average percentage is 12. Thus the combination of unattractive owner-occupancy opportunities and the availability of owner-occupant style units are likely to have produced the group of "potential owners," who as renters in the statistical work are indistinguishable from a large block of owners.

Summary of Findings

1. The relationship between income (current and permanent) and the probability of homeownership was found to be definitely non-linear, with the effect of increments of income generally being positive but at a decreasing rate at the upper end of the range of observed income. For white primary individuals the effect of permanent income on tenure probability actually appears to be negative at the highest levels.
2. Measures of both current and permanent incomes were significant determinants of the probability of homeownership for all but one white household type. The significance of current income likely reflects a combination of errors in estimating permanent income and the importance of transitory incomes in affecting the timing of the home purchase decision. For black households only current income significantly affected the probability of tenure choice.
3. The relationship between the probability of homeownership and most explanatory variables, including income and the number of persons in the household, were found to differ substantially among household types of the same race and between the same household type by race.
4. After controlling for income, family composition, and peer group effects, federal income tax subsidies were found to significantly affect the tenure

---

[s] The greater proportion of black renter households in single unit structures than whites is not attributable to there being more black families among renting households. In fact 84 percent of white renters were families while only 77 percent of black renters were families.

decision only of the two younger husband-wife white household types which also displayed the greatest income elasticity of demand for owner-occupancy. The affects of the tax advantages on homeownership apparently are largely embodied in the affects of income.

5. The models estimated for black household types were not as robust as those for white household types. While this may in part be due to smaller sample sizes and the low degree of variance of some of the explanatory variables, an argument can be made that the ambiguity of the estimated relations reflect the affect of residential racial segregation in limiting the quality of the homeownership opportunities available to black households.

5 Differences in Homeownership Among Metropolitan Areas

Introduction

In the second chapter of this volume the wide variation in the rate of homeownership among metropolitan areas in the United States for individual household types was documented. Given the information on the determinants of homeownership for a single market found in the previous chapter, it is now possible to analyze the between SMSA variation with some confidence. This work thus contrasts with that reported in the last chapter, and for that matter with most prior work on the demand for owner-occupancy, by making the SMSA the unit of observation in the analysis.

To carry out the analysis it is necessary to develop a more rigorous model of the aggregate demand for owner-occupancy than that presented in the third chapter. While greater rigor is achieved, the resultant model is much less detailed in its consideration of non-income factors as determinants of the aggregate tenure decision. The development of the model is presented in the next section. The remainder of the chapter is taken up with the empirical specification, estimation, and evaluation of the model developed. Of particular interest in this work is the comparison of the estimates of the income elasticity of homeownership developed in this chapter with those for the Pittsburgh area households presented in Chapter 4. The results of this chapter provide us with a better basis for comparing the determinants of homeownership by race, as well as other analyses of homeownership which are pursued in the final part of the book.

The Model

We begin once again with the relationship between the probability of being a homeowner, P, and income, Y, for an individual household, holding all other factors fixed. In general, one can imagine that at low levels of income the probability of homeownership is small due to the difficulty of assembling the initial capital and obtaining the necessary credit-risk certification. On the other hand, at high levels of income such difficulties are comparatively minor and the tax subsidies to ownership greater so that the probability of ownership is quite high. It follows that between these two income groups—that is for those households, similarly situated in other ways, who are amassing the necessary savings and credit record attendant with higher but still modest incomes—the

81

sensitivity of the probability of ownership to increments of income is compara-tively greater than at either end of the income distribution. Thus the probability of ownership-income relation, holding other factors fixed, is posited to be of the s-shaped form shown in Figure 3-3, which served as the basis of work in the previous chapter. Algebraically this s-shaped relationship can be represented by

$$P = e^{\alpha - B/Y} \tag{5.1}$$

in which α is the upper limit which P approaches as Y becomes great.

One can think of similar relations existing in the aggregate for whole metropolitan areas. Figure 5-1 depicts the aggregate distribution of the fre-quency of homeownership by income level for two metropolitan areas, A and B. In going from the household to the aggregate relationship in a single city, households with widely differing characteristics have been grouped together. Further, in viewing the aggregate tenure-income relations for two different cities, differences in the characteristics of the two housing markets—prices, structural types, size, etc.—have also been introduced.

Now it would clearly be convenient both expositionally and operationally to be able to summarize in a single measure the host of factors other than income which produce differences in ownership rates between cities. If areas A and B, and the families who lived there were identical except in their incomes, a single

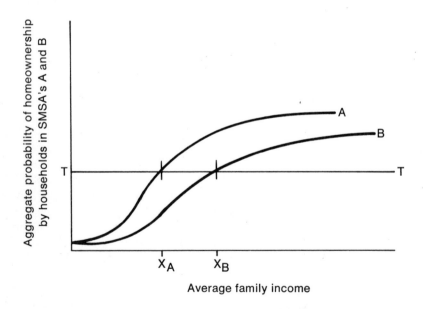

Figure 5-1. The Aggregate Income-Tenure Relationship

curve in Figure 5-1 would suffice; but they are not and there are two curves. In A at practically every income level the frequency of homeownership is greater than in B. One way of summarizing the differences in the two areas is to ask what income level is associated with a given frequency of ownership. In Figure 5-1, for example, the frequency level T is associated with incomes of X_A and X_B in A and B, respectively. The difference, $X_B - X_A$, summarizes the forces making homeownership (at any given income level) less attractive in area B than in Area A.

X_j, then, is the level of income at which households in area j have some specified probability of being an owner-occupant. Influences on X_j include differences in family type, size and composition, characteristics of the housing stock, and other factors which affect the price of owner-occupied housing relative to rental housing. X_j can be thought of as a generalized measure of the cost (in terms of income) of a specified probability of owner-occupancy, or a measure of the effective price of owner-occupancy to the household.

For an individual household within a given market, the ownership decision can be thought of as being determined by the household's income relative to X_j. If T in Figure 5-1 were set at 0.5 or at the average probability of ownership in j, then X_j is an *income of indifference*: above it ownership is more likely; below, rental tenure is the rule.

The income of indifference idea is demonstrated through Figure 5-2, which depicts the relationship between the price of owner-occupied housing services relative to rental housing services (Po/Pr) and income for a given household. Because of the progressive structure of federal income taxes and the better financial terms on mortgages available to the more affluent, the relation is downward sloping. The initial situation is depicted by CC'. At some predefined value of the price ratio, $(Po/Pr)_I$, the household is indifferent between the two forms of tenure; this value has a corresponding income associated with it of X_{j_0}.

Now let there be an increase in (Po/Pr) associated with every level of income, as shown by DD'. Such an increase could result from an increase in demand for owner occupancy—stemming, for example, from a rise in incomes.[a] The household's income of indifference increases to X_{j_1}. Similarly, if (Po/Pr) fell at every income level, due perhaps to an increase in the supply of units "suitable" for owner-occupancy, the income of indifference would fall. In Figure 5-2 this is depicted by EE' and X_{j_2}. The income of indifference can be related to the income-tenure relation (Figure 5-1) by noting that each X_j in Figure 5-2 corresponds to a frequency of homeownership of 0.5 (Figure 5-1); the lower the value of X_j, the lower the level of income at which the city will attain that rate of ownership.

The income-tenure relation for an individual household can be modified to allow for X_j as

---

[a]Note that DD' is the net position; the full shift outward in Po/Pr is partially offset by the increased benefits from federal tax laws. Also we are holding $(Po/Pr)_I$ fixed for simplicity; it could clearly change with the shift of the curve.

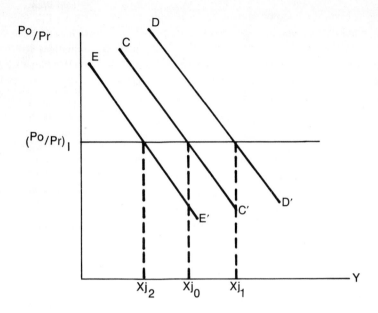

Figure 5-2. Relative Price of Owner-Occupied Housing Services and the "Income of Indifference"

$$P = e^{\alpha - \beta(X_j/Y)} \tag{5.1a}$$

The tenure decision depends on the household's income relative to the income of indifference.

Aggregation of the household tenure-income relation, (5.1a), over all households in city j requires integrating (5.1a) under some assumed distribution. The integration proved intractable under the assumption of a normal distribution, but it was tractable using a log-normal distribution. Consequently, the expression actually integrated is:

$$\overline{lnP} = \int_{-\infty}^{\infty} \left[\alpha - \beta e^{\ln\left(\frac{Y}{X_j}\right)} \right] \left[\frac{e^{-\left[\ln\left(\frac{Y}{X_j}\right) - \overline{\ln\left(\frac{Y}{X_j}\right)}\right]^2 / 2\sigma^2}}{\sqrt{2\pi\sigma^2}} \right] d\ln\left(\frac{Y}{X_j}\right) \tag{5.2}$$

where $\overline{lnP}$ and $\overline{\ln(\frac{Y}{X_j})}$ are logarithms of the geometric means of P and $\frac{Y}{X_j}$ and σ^2 is the variance of $\ln(\frac{Y}{X_j})$. Integration and simplification of (5.2) yields our basic model:

$$\overline{lnP} = \alpha - \beta e^{-\left[\overline{\ln\left(\frac{Y}{X_j}\right)} - \frac{\sigma^2}{2}\right]}$$
(5.3)

There are two advantages to incorporating the horizontal displacement factors (X_j) directly in the income term instead of adding those factors separately into a model determining the probability of ownership. First, it is likely that other functional forms would misspecify the interrelationship between the factors influencing X_j and income.[b] Second, it would be difficult to account for all factors which determine X_j as independent variables both because of data limitations and the interactions among the factors themselves and with income. This is not to suggest that we are disinterested in analyzing the determinants of X_j; indeed this is the focus of the second part of the analysis.

Quite clearly, the between city displacement is the result of the interaction of both supply and demand factors in this housing market. In modeling X_j two approaches were available and experimented with. In the first a full structural model akin to that developed in the final section of Chapter 3 and given in Appendix F was established in which X_j was determined by demand factors, including the price of owned housing relative to rented, the price of housing relative to other goods, and the type and size of families. A supply function was, in turn, written in the price-determining form and made a function of structural characteristics of the housing stock and P. The second approach is a reduced-form of the first in which the price terms are substituted for in the function determining X_j, and P is substituted for in the supply function of owner-occupied housing. Since the second approach generally offered more fruitful results and since the estimates of the structural equations were of only secondary interest to the overall study, the reduced form formulation has been adopted for presentation here.

Specification of Variables

The basic data source was the Fourth Count 1970 Census of Population and Housing as available on magnetic tape.[1] Because the basic model requires a measure of real income and some of the reduced form models include the price of housing and other services, the sample was restricted to the thirty-nine

---

[b]A second specification which did not include X_j in the income term proper was experimented with. Models estimated using the second specification included price and other variables in the function determining P. The results from this specification were always inferior to those obtained when X_j was included in the income term. This confirms the multiplicative nature of the relation between Y and the factors composing X_j and indicates the horizontal displacement in the relation between areas to be of greater importance than the shifts in the intercepts which the second specification captures.

metropolitan areas for which data on the cost of housing and other goods are available on a standardized basis from the Bureau of Labor Statistics.[c]

The most fundamental specification required to estimate the basic function is the definition of X_j. As separate models are estimated for several family types as well as for all households, the definition of X_j had to be flexible enough to be readily applicable to all family types. A definition of X_j as the income at which the frequency of owner-occupancy was 0.5—the provisional definition suggested earlier—failed to meet this requirement, because there were some family types in which the frequency of owner-occupancy exceeded 0.5 for all income classes. Instead, X_j was defined as the income level (in each SMSA) at which the frequency of owner-occupancy corresponds to the average frequency for that family type in all metropolitan areas in the United States. Due to certain data limitations this simple procedure was not, however, strictly followed.[d]

---

[c]The sample cities are listed and the data for 1969 presented in U.S. Bureau of Labor Statistics *3 Budgets for an Urban Family of Four Persons 1969-1970* (Washington, D.C.: U.S. Government Printing Office, 1972). This body of data has been extensively used in other housing studies, e.g., F. de Leeuw "The Demand for Housing: A Review of the Cross-Section Evidence," *Review of Economics and Statistics* 53 (February 1971): 1-10. It should be noted that the price of housing services from the BLS may be biased toward housing occupied by white households. The BLS surveys rents and housing expenditures for the same "standard unit" in each of the metropolitan areas in its sample. Some of the qualifications of the standard unit concern the type of area in which it is located. In part the description of included units reads: "Located in a neighborhood with play space for children . . . ; within 10 blocks of public transportation; and not adjacent to either a refuse dump or more than one of the following hazards: railroads or elevated tracks, noisy or smoke-and fume-developing industrial installations, main traffic activity, or inter-city truck route." In practice this could lead to an undersampling of inner-city neighborhoods in which many blacks are concentrated. The structural qualifications limit the number of units occupied by the poor included, and the poor are disproportionately black. For additional details see, U.S. Bureau of Labor Statistics (H. Lemale and M.S. Stotz), "The Interim City Worker's Family Budget," *Monthly Labor Review*, August 1960, pp. 785-808.

[d]To determine X_j as stated in the text requires knowledge of the incidence of owner-occupancy by income class and by family type. Such data are available by household type for both races combined and for each race aggregated across all household types. It is not, however, available for individual household types by race. For the present estimates the X_j's for white households were assumed to be the same as those for the corresponding X_j's for both races combined. Some bias may be introduced through this assumption; while it is probably negligible overall given the relative importance of white households to all households in most cities, for individual households to all households in most cities, for individual household types some minor bias is possible.

For individual black households separate estimates of the X_j's were used based on differing assumptions as to the relation between the X_j's for blacks and the X_j's for both races combined. The first assumption was that the X_j's are the same for all black households; this is an assumption of no relation between the X_j's for household types of both races combined and those of blacks. The second assumption was that the relation between the X_j's for individual household types and the X_j for all household types combined for both races is the same as the similar relation for black household types and all black households combined.

Formally, let $X_{j_{tt}} = X_j$ of all household for both races combined; $X_{j_{it}} = X_j$ of household type i for both races combined; $X_{j_{tb}} = X_j$ of all black households; $X_{j_{ib}} = X_j$ of black household type i. The β's were estimated under the assumption that for all i, $X_{j_{ib}} = X_{j_{tb}}$. The adjustment to obtain the β's reported in the text is made under the assumption: $X_{j_{it}} / X_{j_{tt}} = X_{j_{ib}} / X_{j_{tb}}$. The first assumption was used in actually estimating the regression models. This

The calculation of $\overline{lnP}$, the log of the geometric mean of the incidence of owner-occupancy over income classes, like X_j requires data on the distribution of tenure by income class by family type which, as explained in footnote d, is not available separately by race from the Census. This was approximated by the log of the arithmetic mean which can be computed from data for aggregate income and the total number of households. Comparison of estimates made using both measures in the models for both races combined indicated little bias is introduced through this approximation.[e] Only estimates using the arithmetic mean are given in the next section.

As noted earlier the basic function, (5.3), is the aggregate counterpart of the tenure choice-income model for an individual household given by (5.1a). Fortunately (5.3) turns out to be a linear relationship of a logarithmic, reciprocal type like (5.1) and (5.1a). Consequently it was possible to estimate the model using the ordinary least squares technique.

For explaining X_j of both races combined one expects *ceteris paribus*, the presence of blacks with their lower average tenure rates to cause X_j to shift upwards. The presence of blacks is measured by three variables: the percentage of households of family type i headed by a black; the percentage of all households in the SMSA headed by blacks; and, the ratio of the first two variables, which gives a measure of the relative importance of blacks in a family type to the entire population.

The spatial distributions of black households have been measured by the well-known Taeuber indices of residential segregation for central cities for 1960[2] and by two measures of relative clustering developed by Masters, also for 1960.[3] The first Masters' measure, *NWT*, is simply the fraction of all black households

assumption, though, is unnecessarily unrealistic. Because of the form of Equation (5.3) it is possible to alter X_j and change β in a compensating manner such that the tenure choice-income relation is unaffected. This procedure has been followed in adjusting the estimated β's for black households (reported in Appendix D) to correspond with the second assumption. The β values reported in Table 5-1 are thus based on the second assumption enumerated above. An unknown bias is introduced through this procedure, but there is little option given the data limitations. These estimates should be roughly comparable with those for both races combined and white households.

A second problem in obtaining the needed values of X_j was caused by extreme rates of owner-occupancy relative to the national average rate in some areas. As an example, if the probability of ownership of indifference (i.e., the national rate) was 0.5 and for some area the ownership rate exceeded 0.5 for this household type at even the lowest income interval given on the Census tape, then an arbitrary value lower than the mid-point of the lowest interval would have to be assigned for X_j to retain the observation in the sample. Instead of making this assignment such observations were dropped from the sample. Attempts to change the definition of the probability of indifference resulted basically in losing observations from the opposite end of the income distribution in exchange for those gained. As a consequence there is some variation in sample sizes, as indicated in Appendix D. The sample for black households consists of the same twenty-nine areas for all household types because X_j for all households combined in the estimates (assumption 1, above) was used in all estimates; most of the omitted observations were due to lack of separate data for black households in the Census data. This variation in samples among household types and race further restricts the direct comparability of the various estimates.

[e]Estimates for both races combined by household type using the geometric mean and the arithmetic mean are presented in Appendix D.

living in census tracts in which more than one-half of the population is black. The second measure, GS/N, is the ratio of weighted average "ghetto size" (with the weights being the black population of the ghettos) divided by the total number of blacks living in all ghettos in the city. Ghettos are groups of contiguous Census tracts each of whose populations is over half black. The measure ranges from zero to one, with one indicating extreme clustering.

The expected direction of the relation between the degree of segregation and homeownership is ambiguous. It might be that a high degree of segregation fosters the development of black financial institutions which could make home financing more readily available. On the other hand, greater segregation could reduce outside financing possibilities to individuals to more than offset the capital available from minority institutions.

Recent analysis by Kain and Quigley has suggested that an important determinant of lower rates of black ownership is the relative dearth of single unit structures available in the areas in which black households are concentrated.[4] To measure this phenomena we have calculated the ratio of the percentage of all occupied units which are single-unit structures to the percentage of all black-occupied units which are in single-unit structures. If one assumes that structural preferences are the same for both races and variation in family types are held fixed, then a high ratio will indicate black households are constrained in their housing structure choice. Since the great majority of owner-occupied units are in single-unit structures, the probability of ownership will be reduced at any given income or X_j increased.

The variables describing the characteristics of the housing stock and market in the supply of housing are generally self-explanatory. They include market size as measured by the number of housing units in the market, the age distribution of the stock, and the distribution of the stock by structure type. In some specifications the effects of these variables have been summarized by the ratio of the price per unit of housing services in the area (P_h) to the price per unit of all other goods (P_t).

Estimates of the Tenure Choice-Income Relationship

The results of estimating the basic model, (5.3), are given in the first three panels of Table 5-1. The estimates are for six household types and for all house types combined for blacks, whites, and both races together. Since all of the estimates are significant at the 1 percent level, the t-ratios and F statistics are excluded from this summary; full estimates are presented in Appendix D.

A cursory examination of the estimates of the α's and β's reveals wide variations among family types within races and substantial variation between races. To put these estimates in perspective the relationships for both races combined for the four husband-wife family types have been plotted in Figure 5-3. The values for X_j assumed for each household type in calculating the relationships are "typical," but there is sharp variation among the SMSAs in their X_j values for each of the household types. The figure illustrates several key features of both the underlying relation and the differences among these household types. The difference between the upper bound which the frequency of ownership approached for the youngest families as compared with the others is dramatic. For all of these families, though, after income reaches about $16,000 the sensitivity of $1nP$ to increments of income is very low. The greatest sensitivity is between the very lowest incomes and about $10,000.[f] Among the family types the high income elasticity of the youngest families and the low elasticity for the eldest households is clearly evident. This is in keeping with our expectations: young families with small savings are typically sensitive to income increases as such increments may provide the margin of savings required for a downpayment; ownership by elderly households on the other hand generally reflects decisions made in the past, often on the basis of greater earnings. The income elasticity of middle-aged families falls between these extremes. Family growth and other pressures make homeownership more imperative for many such households compared to their younger counterparts, and this is reflected in the lower income elasticity. Overall these estimates reflected in the figure emphasize the differences and household types in the tenure choice decision.

Referring to Table 5-1 the patterns just discussed are evident across races. Looking first at the α's, the upper bound to ownership frequency approached at high income levels, non husband-wife families are seen to have values below older husband-wife households for both races. But the α's for primary individuals differ sharply by race; this difference may be due to differences in samples.[g] In three instances the antilog of e^{α} is slightly over 1.0. As suggested by Figure 5-3, this limit is one that is approached *very* slowly so the upper boundaries in these instances are indistinguishable from unity for practical purposes.

Of special interest are the β estimates. In general the β's indicate the effect of

---

[f]Examination of (5.1a) shows that the curve passes through the origin. Thus between no income and a low income level of about $2,000 the curve is extremely steep. The income level (Y) at the point of inflection is $Y = .5BX_j$. For the eldest husband-wife families plotted in the figure this is at $Y = \$153$; for the youngest husband-wife families Y at the point of inflection is $2,340. The passage through the origin and consequence extreme steepness at the lowest income levels tends to bias downward the predictions of ownership frequencies from the model for the lowest incomes; however, since the distribution of homeowners by income class has few households with extremely low-incomes, the overall bias introduced is small. As an example only 8.5 percent of homeowning husband-wife families with heads over age sixty-five had incomes under $2,000 in 1970. For homeowners of all household types combined the figure was 6.9 percent.

[g]As shown in Appendix D, the difference in sample sizes between white and black households for primary individuals was the greatest for any household type, 12 observations in the white model vs. 29 in the black model. (The reason for this difference is outlined in footnote d.) An additional reason for the difference may be that a greater percentage of black primary individual owner-occupants are over age 65 than whites (60 vs. 54 percent).

Table 5-1
Model Estimates, Mean Elasticities, and Comparative Elasticities for Pittsburgh Households by Race and Household Type[a]

	Husband-Wife Families, Head				Other Families	Primary Individuals	All Households
	Under Age 30	Age 30-44	Age 45-65	Over Age 65			
Both Races Combined[a]							
Antilog e^α	.540	1.02	.952	.858	.674	.374	.867
β	.375	.285	.127	.036	.231	.036	.176
Mean elasticity	.514	.238	.114	.035	.208	.100	.181
Homeownership rate	.281	.752	.815	.806	.457	.312	.606
Black Households[a]							
Antilog e^α	.430	.883	.968	1.02	.733	.631	.749
β	.249[b]	.206[b]	.127	.120[b]	.240	.094[b]	.127[b]
Mean elasticity	.411	.228	.194	.133	.198	.411	.267
Homeownership rate	.203	.587	.687	.648	.316	.258	.424
White Households[a]							
Antilog e^α	.561	1.02	.962	.832	.732	.371	.902
β	.369	.272	.127	.053	.263	.031	.192
Mean elasticity	.493	.220	.110	.050	.212	.078	.189
Point elasticity, $Y = \$4,000$	1.44	.875	.474	.126	.513	.115	c
Point elasticity, $Y = \$12,000$	.480	.288	.157	.042	.172	.038	c
Homeownership rate	.291	.776	.829	.808	.504	.314	.628

Individual White
Pittsburgh Households

Point elasticity, $Y = \$4,000$	1.90	.847	.170	.112	.091	.239	c
Point elasticity, $Y = \$12,000$	.786	.576	.211	.154	.232	.189	c
Homeownership rate	.385	.795	.847	.762	.590	.350	.677

[a]All estimated coefficients reported here are significant at 1 percent level; full models appear in Appendix D.

[b]Significantly different from corresponding β for whites at 5 percent level.

[c]Aggregate estimates were not done as part of Pittsburgh study.

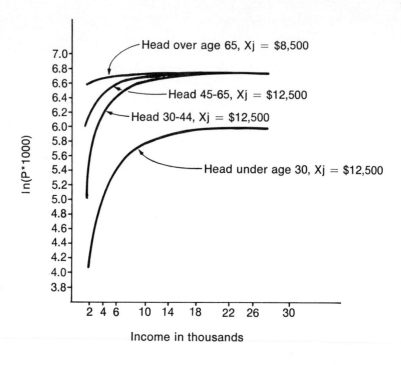

Note: The natural log of 1000, i.e., $\ln$ (1. *1000), is about 6.91.

Figure 5-3. Estimate Homeownership—Income Relations for Four Classes of Husband-Wife Families, Both Races Combined

an increment of income on the probability of owner-occupancy holding other factors causing between city variations in tenure choice fixed. At the income level at which average household income equals the income corresponding to the tenure probability of indifference (that is, the point where $Y = X_j$), β is the elasticity of the probability of owner-occupancy with respect to income. However, since for a number of household types there are substantial differences between mean income and the income level defined as X_j, the elasticities at the means were computed and are shown in the table below the β estimates.

The elasticities demonstrate a wide variation across family types like that observed for the β's: the younger two husband-wife family types and the non-husband-wife household show higher elasticities than other household types. There are appreciable differences between races in the income elasticities. These differences can generally be interpreted as being statistically significant, given the significant differences in β's (indicated in the table) and in incomes and total X_j's between the two races. Excluding primary individuals, the elasticities are higher for black families than for whites for three individual family types and for all family types combined.[h] On balance it seems clear that the elasticity of the frequency of homeownership with respect to income is likely greater for black households than for whites.

It is possible to compare the estimated elasticities for the *white* households just described with elasticities derived from the analysis of tenure choice for Pittsburgh area households presented in Chapter 4. This comparison between the income elasticities based on analysis of individual households and on aggregated observations is of interest given the controversy on the magnitude of the income elasticity of the demand for housing services.[5] The comparison made here may indicate whether this controversy will be carried over into the demand for owner-occupancy.

The comparison is facilitated by the average rates of homeownership for white Pittsburgh household types (shown in the last panel of Table 5-1) being fairly close to the average of those of the cities included in the aggregate analysis. Table 5-1 also contains two-point elasticity estimates for each of the six white household types based on the two analyses (panels 3 and 4). Two-point elasticities are given because the models estimated for the Pittsburgh households employ several different specifications of the basic functional form so that looking only at the mean elasticity or a single point elasticity could be misleading. The elasticities based on a loghyperbolic relation (like that for the aggregate model) decline monotonically as income increases.

The entries in Table 5-1 show that for both sets of point elasticities for the husband-wife household types the elasticities decline steadily as the age of the household head increases. In addition the elasticities at income equal to $4,000 are quite close in magnitude, except for the heads age 45-65. For the same household types, for the elasticities at $Y = \$12,000$ larger differences between the estimates from the two analyses are evident; at this income level the elasticities based on the Pittsburgh sample are all greater than those from the aggregate sample.

The elasticities for the other two household types display much less agreement than those for husband-wife households. In fact the only consistency is the elasticity for primary individuals in the estimates based on the Pittsburgh sample being greater than similar elasticities based on the aggregate sample at both income levels. On balance it appears that while the elasticities of demand for owner-occupancy with respect to income estimated from household and aggregate data are reasonably comparable for "standard" husband-wife house-

---

[h]The elasticities of white households exceed those for blacks for the youngest husband-wife household type and for the "other family" household type. For "other families" this result may stem from the assumption (described in footnote d) made in calculating X_j for blacks. It is quite possible that the X_j of black "other families" may not be related to the X_j of all black households as the X_j of such families of both races. The situation for young black husband-wife families is less apparent but the difference may be associated young blacks being less settled than their white counterparts.

holds, they are quite diverse for non-standard household types. Clearly the previous statement needs to be tempered by the fact that it is based on only a single comparison.

Evaluation of the Basic Model

While the previous section described in some detail the meaning of the estimates and contrasted the estimates by racial groups and household type, it said little about the "quality" of the estimates, save that they are significant at high levels of statistical confidence. Further evaluation is presented here for two reasons. First, it is of interest to know more about how well the tenure choice-income relation is represented by the model estimated, Equation (5.3). Second, since the estimates are the first done across housing markets both with this degree of rigor and for separate households by race, it is likely that they may be employed in policy analysis; and, some additional indication of their characteristics will be useful for those considering their use.

As noted earlier, an examination of the estimated models with their accompanying statistical data indicate the estimated relationships to be statistically valid. The student t statistics and F statistics all indicate significance at the 1 percent level. There is, though, a substantial variance between races and among household types in the degree of the variation in owner-occupancy among cities explained by the regression models. Table 5-2 shows the range of the coefficients of determination adjusted for degrees of freedom for these models. The range is substantial. Better fits were generally obtained for husband-wife households than for other families and primary individuals; the fits for black households were less good than for whites for four of the six household types.

In order to determine if there is a systematic misspecification in the relation depicted in Equations (5.1) and (5.3), the rates of owner-occupancy determined using the estimated model for all households combined were plotted on the same graph with the actual relations. Figure 5-4 displays these predicted and actual relations for five widely diverse metropolitan areas. The single prediction line for two pairs of areas (Pittsburgh—Portland and Austin—Durham) results from X_j

Table 5-2
Adjusted $\bar{R}^2$'s from Tenure Models

	Separate Household Type Models		Model for All
	Lowest $\bar{R}^2$	Highest $\bar{R}^2$	Households Combined
Both races combined	.36	.89	.67
Black households	.30	.58	.56
White households	.42	.90	.70

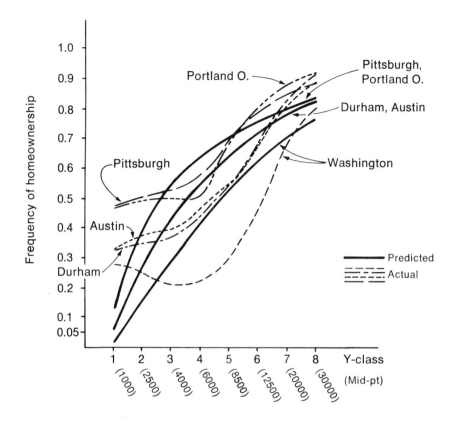

Figure 5-4. Actual and Predicted Ownership-Income Relation, Selected Cities, All Households Combined

being the same for each pair of areas. From the figure it is evident that for households with incomes below the $3,000-$5,000 interval (interval 3), the predicted tenure frequencies are systematically below the actual. As noted in the previous section (footnote f) this stems basically from the mathematical properties of the basic model. The difference between the predicted and actual tenure rates diminishes rapidly after the third interval.

The impact of the systematic under prediction at the lowest income levels is suggested by Figure 5-5, which shows distribution of white and black owner-occupant households in American metropolitan areas in 1970. A glance shows that a substantially greater portion of black homeowners have incomes under $5,000 than do whites: roughly 31 percent of blacks versus 17 percent of whites. It seems probable that this difference in income distributions is responsible for the comparatively low explanatory power of the tenure choice-income model for black households.

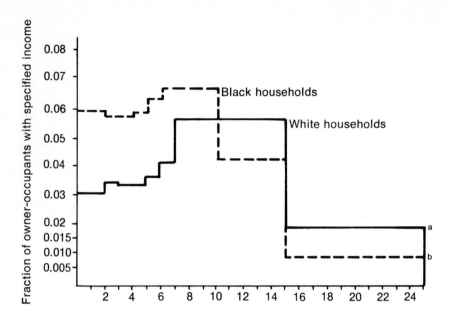

[a]7.0 percent of white owner-occupants had incomes over $25,000.

[b]1.8 percent of black owner-occupants had incomes over $25,000.

Source: Table B-7 and B-17 of U.S. Bureau of the Census, Census of Housing: *1970 Metropolitan Housing Characteristics*, Final Report, HC(2)-1, (Washington, D.C.: U.S. Government Printing Office, 1972).

Figure 5-5. Distribution of Owner-Occupants in U.S. SMSAs by Level of Income

It is possible to further explore the aggregate tenure choice-income relation by making use of additional data which is available only for all households combined; specifically, this is data on joint distribution of tenure and income. (The data used to make the estimates of the previous section, it will be recalled, were the *average* ownership rate and the income *distribution* for each household type in each SMSA.) The first step in this exploration was to plot the scatter of tenure rate-income points; in making this plot, illustrated in Figure 5-6, income was divided by X_j in order to place all observations on the same basis, i.e., to abstract from the host of non-income factors which cause tenure to vary among cities. The 40 points (8 tenure-income class observations for each of five cities) were also used to fit several functional forms which would presumably provide a smaller error because of the greater information being utilized for each area. The results, presented in Table 5-3, show that these simple models fit the data better than the model estimated in the previous section. The quadratic model does particularly well.

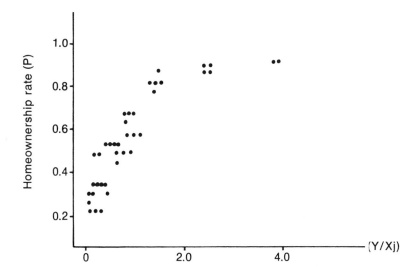

Figure 5-6. Income Versus Y/X_j, All Households Combined

Whereas the models based on greater information would likely offer better predictions of aggregate household tenure rate given an income level especially for low incomes, there are nevertheless two reasons why the estimates of the previous section remain quite serviceable. The first is that the basic aggregate model given by (5.3) has a direct individual household analog, and thus it is possible to apply the information derived from the aggregate model directly to the study of the behavior of individual households. No such claim can be made for the simple models shown in Table 5-3. The second reason for the serviceability of the earlier estimates is that the Bureau of Census has not made available data of the type used in this section for individual household types by race. Given the great variance among household types in the parameters of the model estimated in the previous section, the need for disaggregation by race and household type is quite evident.

Reduced Form Estimates of X_j

Recall that in this analysis X_j is the real level of household income in area j at which households have the same rate of homeownership as the average of all households in metropolitan areas in the United States. As stated earlier, when the model for X_j is expressed as a reduced form, the variation in X_j among areas summarizes the demand and supply forces causing tenure to vary among areas. Note that X_j is not a residual from the estimated models presented in the

Table 5-3
Measures of Predictive Powers of Selected Tenure Choice Models

	Measures of goodness of Fit[c]		
	Mean Absolute Error	RMSE	$\bar{R}^2$
Model Type			
1. Models estimated using tenure rates by income class and Y/X_j data[a]			
a. Ten = 373 + .202Y/X_j	.084	.102	.756
b. Ten = 526 + 171 $1n\ (Y/X_j)$	.074	.092	.801
c. Ten = 271 + .459 Y/X_j − 8.2 × $10^{-5}\ (Y/X_j)^2$	.048	.067	.893
2. Basic tenure model,[b] fit to 39 cities	.100	.133	.665

Note: Models estimated across all household types.

[a]Ten = (tenure rate) *1000., Y/X_j = (income/income of indifference) *1000

[b]Model is of form $1nP = X − \beta\ (X_j/Y)$

[c]Mean absolute error and root mean squared error (RMSE) measure error between actual and predicted tenure rates by income class. R^2 is a measure of the goodness of fit between the actual tenure rate and the independent variable(s).

previous section. In brief X_j is simply a different measure of tenure variation, but it is the one which is essential to our statement of an estimable tenure-income model.

Four groups of independent variables have been used to explain the variation in X_j: (1) a group accounting for variations in the distribution of households by size, by composition, and by household type; (2) a group accounting for variations in market size and in the distribution of the vintage and of structural types of the housing stock; (3) a group measuring the relative importance and spatial distribution of black households in the SMSA; and (4) mean household income.

The expected signs of the coefficients for those variables lowering the demand for owner-occupancy or increasing the supply of "suitable" units should be negative in the model explaining X_j—opposite from that which they should have on the probability of owner-occupancy. For variables increasing the demand for owner-occupancy or decreasing the supply of "suitable" units a positive relation with X_j is expected.

Estimates of multiple regression models explaining X_j for both races combined by family type are presented in Table 5-4.[i] The independent variables listed in the table are only a few of a large number of different variables and

[i]Table 5-4 does not contain an estimated model for the primary individual family type since there were only twelve cities for which X_j could be defined. See fn. d for further explanation.

specifications tried. Even with this considerable experimentation, however, generally only about 40 percent of the variance in X_j was explained—much less than the variation in tenure explained by the summary income models presented in the previous section. This underscores the potential inaccuracy and difficulties in obtaining a good income-tenure probability estimate from using a model in which income and the determinants of X_j entered in an additive fashion.[j]

One aspect of the results which is particularly striking is that mean household income (variable 13) is a significant determinant of X_j for only the most elderly husband-wife family type and for all family types combined. As expected, higher incomes are associated with higher levels of X_j. But for both of the family types for which it was significant, income has an extremely powerful effect, one which a priori seems to be implausible.[k] Also, in these models the strength of the income effect served to significantly reduce the effect which the housing stock variables had on X_j.[l]

A second notable aspect of the results is the performance of the structure type variable. As the results indicate, the most consistently significant variable is the presence of units in single unit structures in 1960.[m] For three of the household types, each percentage point increase reduces the household income necessary for an area to reach the national ownership rate by over $270; for these household types the elasticity of X_j with respect to the percentages of units in single unit structures is near one when evaluated at the means of both variables. The availability of suitable owner-occupied structures is an important determinant of X_j for all but the husband-wife households with head age 30-44, a group for whom the demand for owner-occupancy is apparently less dependent on the availability of particular structure types.

---

[j]We were not satisfied with the low explanatory power of these models and consequently advanced and tested several hypotheses which might account for more of the variance. Since our confidence in the theoretical validity of these hypotheses is not as great as it is for those underlying the models presented in Table 5-4, the discussion of these additional hypotheses is in Appendix E.

[k]A coefficient of the income variable of greater than 1 implies declining homeownership over time; for a coefficient of less than 1 increasing ownership is indicated. Evidently neither situation could realistically be sustained indefinitely. The expected value of the income coefficient was, therefore, unity. In the models in which the income term is significant, the coefficient of income differs significantly from 1. In Appendix E models with additional independent variables have been tested for X_j for all households combined. In some of these more complete models, the coefficient of income is not significantly different from 1. Both this and the generally low R^2's of the models given in Table 5-4 suggest that the models in Table 5-4 are not completely specified. The high coefficient of income might easily be accounted by this specification problem.

[l]The simple relation between X_j and income was significant for all family types. The lack of significance of income in the models for several of the family types after controlling for the other independent variables implies that for these households the characteristics of the stock available, which are significantly correlated with mean income, simply dominate income as determinants of X_j.

[m]"Single-unit structures" include both attached and detached single-unit structures. Several different specifications of suitable or desired owner-occupied units were calculated which included varying fractions of the number of units in two-, three-, and four-unit structures together with single-unit structures. These specifications were all correlated above 0.9, so the simplest definition, the fraction in one-unit structures, was used.

Table 5-4
Regression Analysis of X_j, Both Races Combined by Household Type[a]

	Husband-Wife Families, Head				Other Families	All Households
	Under Age 30	Age 30-44	Age 45-65	Over Age 65		
Constant	33126 (2.93)[c]	20480 (1.72)	29813 (2.01)	-64413 (2.05)	-5048 (.70)	-20808 (1.08)
1. Fract. H-W[b] households with 2-3 persons		-3934 (.22)		82608 (2.69)		
2. Fract. H-W[b] households with 5 or more persons			34423 (.98)			
3. Fract. of female headed households under age 65					22215 (2.56)	
4. Percent of housing units in 1-unit structures, 1960	-295.8 (2.81)	-89.4 (1.42)	-273.2 (2.08)	-285.3 (2.01)	-92.5 (2.31)	-78.5 (1.08)
5. Percent of housing units built 1939 or earlier	-55.3 (.85)	-113.5 (2.45)	-228.3 (3.15)	-76.1 (.76)		-84.4 (1.79)
6. Number of occupied housing units in SMSA	.0006 (.36)	.0012 (1.18)	.0020 (1.12)	.0029 (1.64)	.0014 (2.20)	-.0017 (1.36)
7. No. of black households of family type i as fract. of white household of type i	12924 (1.00)	5158 (1.69)			1809 (1.38)	
8. Percent households in SMSA headed by a black			34.0 (.25)			-53.3 (.52)
9. Ratio: percent all occupied units in 1-unit struct. to percent black-occupied units in 1-unit structures			2165 (1.05)	4499 (2.60)		
10. Fract. of households type i black headed/(fract. all households black headed)	5683. (1.75)					

	(1)	(2)	(3)	(4)	(5)	(6)
11. No. "other family" households as fraction of all households						84736 (1.70)
12. No. primary individuals as fraction of all households						39287 (1.56)
13. Mean household income				4.56 (3.78)		2.17 (2.94)
$\bar{R}^2$	.380	.363	.328	.760	.386	.406
F	5.41	5.11	3.77	12.6	6.51	4.52

[a]Table excludes the primary individual household type, but these households are included in the "all households" results.

[b]Husband-wife.

[c]t-ratios in parentheses.

The age of the housing stock was a highly significant determinant of X_j for two family types and of marginal significance for all households combined. There are two non-mutually exclusive interpretations of this finding. One is that older SMSAs (which generally have older housing stocks) have had a tradition of homeownership and that this tradition continues to be pervasive. Note that size of the area and availability of suitable structures are being held fixed. The alternative interpretation is that older units are less expensive to purchase since they will provide a shorter stream of services than newer units. This makes possible home purchases by lower income households. It is not possible to clarify the interpretation with the data at hand, although the frequent exceptions to the first interpretation, such as Boston, tend to emphasize the second.

The size of housing market, as measured by the number of occupied housing units in the SMSA has a marginally significant influence on X_j for elderly husband-wife families, "other families" and all households combined. The insignificance for younger husband-wife families, especially those with heads between thirty and forty-five, probably reflects the preference of these families for traditional owner-occupied homes and their willingness to live in distant suburban areas if necessary in order to have a house with yard for their families.

Not anticipated was the general insignificance of the effect of family size and family type variables after accounting for variation in X_j due to housing stock characteristics, incomes, and market size. This result for the family type variables in the model explaining X_j for all households combined likely stems from the relatively small variation in the mix of family types across the sample cities.[n]

The racial variables, while generally not statistically significant at high levels of confidence, do indicate definite directions of some relationships. The three variables measuring the relative importance of black households (Nos. 7, 8, and 10 in Table 5-4 described above), all show an increase in the average income required to reach the national ownership rate with an increase in the relative importance of black households. This is consistent with the lower average tenure rates of black households. These increases are not significant for all households combined, though, despite the sizable increases evident for several household types. On balance the results indicate that after controlling for variations in market size and characteristics of the housing stocks X_j will rise (and homeown-

[n]The coefficients of variation for the fraction of all households accounted for by each family type are:

Husband-Wife Families, Head

under age 30	18.5	Non-Husband-Wife families	13.1
age 30-44	7.49	Primary Individuals	13.4
age 45-65	8.41		
over age 65	16.1		

ership decline) with the relative importance of blacks to the total population. Further, for the two elderly husband-wife family types these results show some evidence that supply restrictions on single unit structures to blacks further increase X_j.

It is not the intention of this chapter to analyze the variation in the relative rates of homeownership of white and black households across SMSAs, which is the subject of Chapter 6; but it is nonetheless instructive to examine the determinants of the X_j's of all black households combined to see if the same factors are important in explaining X_j for them as for the entire population.[o] This examination seems particularly warranted when the very low and insignificant correlation between the X_j's of all black households combined. Several differences between these estimates (Table 5-5) and those for all households (Table 5-4) are immediately evident. The vintage of the stock had no significant influence on the X_j of black households, possibly because there is little correspondence between the vintage of the entire stock and that available to blacks. The size of the housing market consistently and significantly increases the income level at which the national rate of homeownership is obtained. Also unlike the results for all households of both races combined, the mean level of

Table 5-5
Regression Analysis of X_j for All Black Households Combined

	(1)	(2)	(3)	(4)
Constant	24979 (2.56)[b]	28415 (2.65)	27196 (2.26)	25606 (2.49)
No. of "other family" households as a fraction of all households	67861 (2.26)	65499 (2.15)	70795 (2.22)	65932 (2.08)
Percent of housing units in single-unit structures, 1960	−348.1 (4.26)	−367.5 (4.28)	−342.4 (4.02)	−353.6 (4.08)
No. of occupied housing units in SMSA	.0027 (2.24)	.0025 (2.01)	.0026 (2.09)	.0026 (2.11)
Percent of households in SMSA headed by blacks				24.3 (.23)
GS/N[a]		−1839 (.79)		
Taeuber index of residential segregation			−38.0 (.33)	
$\bar{R}^2$		.603	.597	.456	.587
F		15.2	11.4	8.82	10.9

[a]See text for explanation (p. 88).

[b]t-statistics in parentheses.

[o]The comparison is with the X_j for all households instead of those for whites alone because the X_j for whites and all households were assumed to be the same, as indicated in fn. d.

household incomes of black households had no significant effect on the level of X_j.

As the estimated models demonstrate, neither the importance of black households relative to all households nor the spatial distribution of black households as measured here were a significant determinant of X_j. Further, although not shown, the variable measuring the restriction of single unit dwellings to black households was insignificant *after* controlling for the percentage of all units in single unit structures throughout the market. The results indicate that the variation in X_j of all black households is not determined, at least directly, by the variation in relative importance of black households or residential segregation. This is not to say, however, that residential segregation may not indirectly influence the coefficients of the market size and housing stock characteristics variables. Nor is it to say that the effects of segregation on X_j (and tenure) may not be quite invariant across areas and thus not evident in the regression results.

The above results confirm that the determinants of X_j for black households are different from those for all households; black households are responding differently to the same broad market forces from whites. How much of this is attributable to residential segregation or discrimination is unclear. However, the results from the previous section which suggest that black households have different income elasticities of owner-occupancy imply that they may also differ in their response to other economic phenomena.

Summary of Findings

The principal findings of this chapter concern the income elasticity of demand for owner-occupancy. The elasticity evaluated at the means for all households combined is about 0.18. Elasticities larger than this were found for the two husband-wife family types with heads under age forty-five and for non-husband-wife family types and for primary individuals. There are substantial differences between races in the elasticities, although the overall pattern for family types just described remains generally valid for both races. The mean income elasticity of all black households combined is somewhat larger than for white households (0.25 vs. 0.19).

Differences in market factors among areas causing variations in tenure were summarized in the variable X_j, the average household income at which households in an urban area j attained the national average rate of homeownership. Estimates of a reduced form model of X_j indicate that variations in X_j were most significantly related to variations in the characteristics of the housing stock, the size of the market, and mean household income. In particular, the percentage of units in single-unit structures and the percentage of units built before 1940 reduce the income required to attain the average national tenure rate. Estimated models of X_j for both races combined indicate a positive association between the relative importance of black households relative to all households and X_j, after controlling for variations in other market factors.

Part III:
Policy Analyses

6

Determinants of the Rate of Homeownership of Black Households Relative to White Households

Introduction

Until very recently studies of the economic effects of residential racial segregation were focused on two issues: (1) whether segregation and possible associated discrimination causes black households to pay higher prices per unit of housing services than white households;[1] and (2) whether segregation has placed blacks at a disadvantage in the labor market because of the location of jobs away from black enclaves.[2] A third issue recently brought to the fore is that of the effect of discrimination on the rate of homeownership of black households relative to whites.[3] This chapter is concerned explicitly with the third issue, and in analyzing it the model developed in the previous chapter is extended. More specifically it seeks to quantify the determinants of the relative rates of homeownership by black households and to assess the role of residential segregation and/or discrimination as a determinant.

That this is a significant social issue was confirmed by the data presented in Chapter 2 which show black households at every income level having substantially lower rates of homeownership. In addition, the prior chapter confirmed that blacks have income elasticities of demand for ownership at least as large as those of their white counterparts.

There are three distinct forms of welfare costs which the forces producing lower homeownership rates may impose on blacks. The first is an increase in the price of owner-occupied housing. This cost can occur because of the effective segmenting of the housing market into black and white sectors, with those dwellings most suitable for owner-occupancy in the black sector commanding a premium. Even in the absence of such segmentation, however, if the stock in the segregated portion of the market were poorly suited to homeownership, greater search costs and/or possible discriminatory mark-ups to an individual black household in a dominantly white neighborhood could raise the price of owner-occupancy.[4] The second welfare cost is a reduction in the extent of household choice regarding tenure; this cost can be closely related to the first since the higher price of owner-occupancy effectively restricts choice.

The third welfare cost, which in the long run may be the most significant, is the reduction in wealth accumulation by blacks. As noted in Chapter 3, the data compiled by Projector and Weiss show homeownership to be very important in the wealth position of low income households. The importance of owner-occupancy in wealth accumulation is also reflected in figures on the debt positions of

109

husband-wife families compiled by Duran Bell using the 1967 Survey of Economic Opportunity data file. The debt positions of both black and white households were found to differ dramatically by form of tenure, regardless of the residential location of the households within the SMSA; owner-occupants showed five to six times the debt of renter households, and analysis of the composition of this debt reveals homeownership to be the major difference.[5] Wealth accumulates to the owner-occupants as they make their mortgage payments.[a] Bell, among others, has stressed the importance of this form of forced savings in the process of wealth accumulation. This debt pattern holds for all income classes included in Bell's analysis.

Against this background analysis of the relative rates of homeownership of white and black households takes on a genuine sense of urgency. The major contribution in this area to date is that by John Kain and John Quigley. Since theirs is the most widely known analysis, it is appropriate to review it in some detail and to use it as a context in which to place the present work.[6] After mustering evidence based on St. Louis households to support the hypothesis that blacks have lower probability of homeownership than whites when controlling for important economic differences between the races, Kain-Quigley analyze the variation in the difference between expected and actual black ownership rates across cities. The expected black ownership rate is computed "by multiplying a matrix of white ownership rates (stratified into income and family size groups) by the income and family size distribution of black households." The differences between expected and actual black rates are then related, using multiple regression analysis, to variables indicating restrictions to blacks in the supply of housing suitable for owner-occupancy.

The average difference between the actual white and black ownership rates as of 1960 for the eighteen cities in their sample is 0.30 (0.65 − 0.35). The difference between the actual white and the expected black rates is 0.11 (0.65 − 0.54), and the authors conclude, "the residual difference, .19, must be attributable to other factors, including the differences in supply restrictions among areas."

One limitation of the Kain-Quigley analysis is that it does not yield estimates of the effects which increments of income versus increments of desegregation or reduction in discrimination would have at the margin on the relative ownership rates of black households. Such estimates are clearly a necessary input for policy considerations.

The purpose of this chapter is not to evaluate the Kain-Quigley analysis or to reanalyze their data in detail. Rather it is to present an alternative analysis of the demand for owner-occupancy of blacks relative to whites in a conventional framework in order to assess the marginal effect of a relative increase in the income of blacks on the tenure decision. Simultaneous with the assessment of the role of income the effects of discrimination are examined.

---

[a] Capital appreciation and income derived through the tax advantages of homeownership may also contribute to wealth accumulation.

The results of pursuing this analysis indicate that the mean income of black households, the price of owner-occupied housing which they face, and the level and variance in the income of white households are significant determinants of the relative rate of homeownership of blacks across cities. A percentage increase in the mean level of black households' incomes produce a larger increase in the relative rate of black homeownership than an equivalent reduction in the price of owner-occupied housing they face. Although significant effects of within market discrimination against blacks leading to higher prices of owner-occupied housing are found, we are unable to associate this price premium with measures of residential segregation or to find direct support for the Kain-Quigley supply restriction hypothesis.

The remainder of the chapter consists of four sections. The following section extends the model of household tenure choice developed in the previous chapter into an aggregate model of relative black/white tenure choice. The next section briefly treats some specification issues and describes the pattern of ownership in the sample cities. The estimated models, based on the data described in the previous chapter, appear in the next section. The final section discusses several implications of these results for public policies.

Extension of the Aggregate Model

We begin with Equation (5.3) from Chapter 5, the aggregate tenure choice-income relation developed and tested in the last chapter:

$$\overline{\ln P} = \alpha - \beta e^{-\left[\overline{\ln (Y/X_j)} - (1/2)\sigma^2\right]}$$

where all symbols are as before. The task now is to formulate a model of relative homeownership for black versus white households. To do this we begin with a simple model of aggregate homeownership, which is stated in the following four functions consisting of a demand function for owner occupancy and a function determining X_j for each race.

$$\overline{\ln P(b)}_j = a_1 - a_2 e^{-\left[\ln (\overline{Y_b}/X_{jb}) - (1/2)\sigma_b^2\right]} \tag{6.1a}$$

$$X_{jb} = b_0 + b_1 Z_j + b_2 SEG_j + b_3 Fb_j \tag{6.1b}$$

$$\overline{\ln P(w)}_j = c_1 - c_2 e^{-\left[\ln (\overline{Y_w}/X_{jw}) - (1/2)\sigma_w^2\right]} \tag{6.2a}$$

$$X_{jw} = d_0 + d_1 Z_j + d_2 F_{wj} \tag{6.2b}$$

$P(b)$ and $P(w)$ are the aggregate probabilities of black and white homeownership in market j. Z is a vector of characteristics of the housing stock and housing market; SEG is a vector of measures of residential racial segregation and/or its effects; F is a vector of family characteristics such as type (husband-wife families vs. non-husband-wife families vs. individuals) and size.

The separate X_j's for each race reflect differences in the income level at which each race obtains the specified rate of homeownership. One can think of A and B in Figure 5-1 as referring to white and black households within the same city instead of all households in separate cities. Thus while the X_j for all households in j will account for *between* city variations in the host of factors other than income which affect tenure choice, the difference between X_{jb} and X_{jw} will summarize non-income factors *within* the SMSA which produce differences in tenure rates by race including various forms of discrimination.

The models as written in (6.1) and (6.2) appear to imply independent submarkets for each race; they are linked, however, by both races facing the same stock of housing (Z_j). It can be argued that blacks are restricted in their housing choice; whites, though, could presumably bid for housing anywhere in the market, and it is in this way that the markets are joined. (Even if it is contended that blacks only get "residual" housing, the residual depends on what is available overall, i.e., on Z_j.)

The models depicted by (6.1) and (6.2) are recursive in that ownership is determined in part by X_j, but X_j in turn is not a function of the rate of ownership. This causality assumption is made for convenience of estimation, and we suspect that in this essentially exploratory work it will not damage the confidence in the type of inference drawn from the estimates. Some reduced-form estimates are, however, presented later which provide an alternative for the reader concerned by this problem.

The functions determining the X_j's are clearly reduced forms since the X_j's depend on the relative price of housing services vs. other goods and the price of owner-occupied housing relative to renter-occupied. In the models reported here, the price terms have been substituted for using the characteristics of the stock and market size. In this formulation X_{jw} depends on the characteristics of the housing stock and of the market itself (e.g., its size) and on the family type and household composition. X_{jb}, on the other hand, depends on the same factors and on the strength of discriminatory practices. These practices are represented by *possible* manifestations of discrimination such as residential segregation.

Equations (6.1) and (6.2) are combined by subtracting (6.2a) from (6.1a) and (6.2b) from (6.1b). This, with some manipulation, yields:

$$\ln[P(b)/P(w)] = \tau_0 - \tau_1 [(X_b/Y_b)\,e^{.5\sigma_b^2} - (X_w/Y_w)\,e^{.5\sigma_w^2}] \qquad (6.3a)$$

$$X_b - X_w = (b_0 + d_0) + (b_1 - d_1)Z + b_2\,SEG + b_3 F_b - d_2 F_w \qquad (6.3b)$$

where the j subscripts, denoting the city, have been omitted. This represents the basic model to be estimated. Because the independent variable in (6.3a) summarizes the effects of a number of variables, it has been attempted in the actual estimates to disentangle the effects of the level of income, the dispersion of income, and the relative price of housing. An important issue in this regard is the sensitivity of these phenomena to the specification in (6.3a). This is explored in a later section.

In (6.3b) the difference between the X's by race are shown to depend on the characteristics of the housing stock of the entire market. In some ways these characteristics will simply reflect differences in the price of housing services between markets. A higher price of housing services, though, would affect the demand of blacks more than proportionately because of the higher uncompensated price elasticity of demand for necessities by the poor in general. Beyond this, individual characteristics of the stock may have important effects. For example, smaller or older owner-occupant units may sell for less which would make them available to less affluent households. The lower initial outlay for such units may be particularly important. In the estimated models, both the individual characteristics and the overall price of housing services are tested.

Statistical Specification and
Sample Description

While the data and variable specification used here are generally the same as those employed in Chapter 5, a few modifications should be noted. First, the present estimates have not been made for separate household types, but rather only for all household types combined. Thus the rate of homeownership used to calculate the X's was the average aggregate ownership rate for all households in all U.S. metropolitan areas in 1970, 59 percent. Thus X is defined as that income at which the households (of a given race) have a homeownership rate of at least 59 percent. The sample was restricted to the twenty-nine SMSAs for which BLS collects price data and which met certain criteria noted in the previous chapter, especially the availability of separate data for black households.[b]

In addition to the variables used in the prior estimates, six family type variables have been included to account for variation in demand for ownership arising from variation in family types. Each of these variables is defined as the ratio of the fraction of black households who are in family type i to the fraction of all white households in the same family type. The six family types included four age groups of husband-wife families, "other" families, and primary individuals.

Finally, the central hypothesis tested by Kain-Quigley was that supply restrictions, particularly access to financing, real estate experts, and neighbor-

[b]See footnote d, Chapter 5.

hoods with housing especially desirable for owner-occupancy has been a major cause of lower homeownership rates among blacks. Following Kain-Quigley, in calculating a measure of the restrictions blacks face the basic assumption has been that strong limitations of these types of access should make themselves evident in lower rates of occupancy of the typical, owner-occupant preferred structures—the single unit dwelling—by blacks than by the community at large. Accordingly, the following two measures were computed:

> SNGUOWN — the ratio of one-unit structures occupied by black owner-occupants to all the structures occupied by black owner-occupants divided by the ratio of one-unit structures occupied by all owner-occupants of all structures occupied by owner-occupants.
>
> SNGUTOT — the ratio of one-unit structures occupied by blacks to all units occupied by blacks divided by the ratio of all one-unit structures to all occupied units.

While the latter measure (which was used in the last chapter) is more general, it should be correlated with the relative ownership rate, simply because owners in general prefer single unit structures. For this reason we emphasize SNGUOWN in the present estimates. A low value of SNGUOWN will indicate black households are constrained in their household choice, if one assumes structural preferences are the same for both races and if variations in family type are held fixed.

Statistics on the lower rate of homeownership of black households compared to white households of the same income level and of the same household type were presented in Chapter 2, and demonstrated that substantial differences exist between the races. Some summary evidence on this same point for all households combined for the twenty-nine metropolitan areas in the present sample is given in Table 6-1. The table shows homeownership rates, average household incomes, and X_j separately for black and white households. In the final two columns it also lists two previously described measures of racial segregation in these SMSAs as of 1960.

Several interesting observations emerge from these data. First, in five areas (Baltimore, Milwaukee, Pittsburgh, Chicago, and Cincinnati) the ownership rate of whites is about double that of blacks; in Hartford the difference is nearly three to one. Only in Austin are rates roughly equivalent, which in part may reflect the extremely high rate of growth of households of moderate incomes in the area over the decade. The second point concerns the income level at which each race would reach the average ownership rate for all metropolitan areas combined (i.e., X_j). Only in Austin is X_{jb} less than X_{jw}. In ten of the sample SMSAs the value of X_j for blacks and whites is the same; but the other eighteen areas X_{jb} is greater, and in some instances by large amounts. The most dramatic example of this last point is for Chicago where X_{jb} exceeds X_{jw} by nearly $20,000. Further, even a quick contrast of the variation in incomes and X_j by race reveals that the variation in X_{jb} exceeds the variation in black incomes

Table 6-1
Selected Variables for Twenty-nine Sample SMSAs, 1970

SMSA	Ownership rate		Income[a] ($000)		X_j[a] ($000)		Segregation measures[b]	
	Black	White	Black	White	Black	Total	GS/N	Taeuber
Atlanta	.40	.62	8.4	15.0	15.8	15.8	.30	93.6
Austin	.53	.55	7.3	12.6	11.1	16.3	1.0	93.1
Baltimore	.32	.65	8.6	13.0	22.7	14.2	.44	89.6
Baton Rouge	.56	.70	7.0	13.7	10.5	10.5	.48	83.9
Chicago	.26	.58	8.8	13.3	32.5	13.5	.83	92.6
Cincinnati	.33	.64	7.5	12.4	23.6	10.0	.35	89.0
Cleveland	.40	.66	8.3	12.8	13.4	13.4	.78	91.3
Dallas	.45	.62	7.6	13.7	15.2	15.2	.51	94.6
Dayton	.51	.68	10.1	13.7	14.9	14.9	.98	91.3
Denver	.46	.62	8.5	12.4	14.6	14.6	1.0	85.5
Detroit	.52	.76	9.7	14.4	14.2	9.7	.74	84.5
Durham	.41	.58	7.1	11.8	14.8	14.8	.40	92.7
Hartford	.22	.62	8.1	13.0	20.8	13.0	1.0	82.1
Houston	.48	.62	7.7	14.0	15.6	15.6	.22	93.7
Indianapolis	.49	.67	8.5	12.2	13.9	9.4	.50	91.6
Kansas City	.56	.67	7.7	12.2	9.6	9.6	.66	90.8
Los Angeles	.38	.50	8.7	12.6	23.0	14.4	.86	81.8
Milwaukee	.33	.62	8.0	11.9	21.1	13.2	1.0	88.1
Minneapolis	.42	.66	8.0	12.5	22.1	13.8	.62	84.0
Nashville	.41	.66	7.4	12.5	15.9	10.6	.74	91.7
Orlando	.50	.73	6.0	12.6	10.8	7.6	.76	98.0
Philadelphia	.49	.71	8.2	12.6	13.9	9.4	.28	87.1
Pittsburgh	.38	.70	7.2	11.8	14.7	10.0	.35	84.6
St. Louis	.39	.69	7.6	12.5	22.8	9.7	.65	90.5
San Diego	.44	.57	7.7	10.8	13.2	13.2	1.0	81.3
San Francisco	.37	.53	8.6	12.7	22.2	13.9	.12	69.3
Seattle	.50	.65	9.2	12.9	14.2	9.7	1.0	79.7
Washington, D.C.	.31	.50	9.6	15.2	21.8	21.8	.94	79.7
Wichita	.48	.66	7.6	11.6	14.5	10.1	1.0	91.9

[a]Adjusted for regional cost of living differences using BLS intermediate budget for family of four.
[b]For 1960.

to a much greater degree than the variation in X_{jw} exceeds the variation in incomes of white households.

Finally, the two measures of racial segregation are of interest because of their divergence. Whereas the Taeubers measure segregation on a block-by-block basis, the index GS/N developed by Masters is based on Census tracts and is focused on the intensity of segregation by measuring the proportion of blacks living in "ghettos" (see Chapter 5 for a full description). In only a few SMSAs are the two measures close, and for areas like Atlanta, Houston, Philadelphia, and San Francisco there is little agreement. These data point up the difficulty of measuring "segregation," and these measurement problems are likely to affect the clarity of the results obtained in estimating the model.

The Estimated Models

Estimates of the basic model of relative ownership rates are presented in Table 6-2. The first column of the table contains the estimate of the model given by (6.3a), that in which mean household income, the dispersion of household incomes, and the income level at which households in a city reach the national rate of homeownership (i.e., X) all enter in a multiplicative fashion. The intercept in the first model has a similar interpretation to that of α in (5.1), namely it is the upper bound which the rate of black homeownership relative to that of whites approaches as incomes of both races become large. The antilog of the coefficient divided by 1000 is 0.88. So even at upper income levels equality in the probability of ownership does not exist.

The independent variable is highly significant and of the expected sign. (Recall that the basic relationship is a reciprocal one between ownership and income; hence a minus sign for an increase in the relative income of blacks.) However, much information as to the separate effects of the various components of the independent variable on relative ownership rates is suppressed in this form. The models in columns 2-4 separate the components of this variable.

The regression models in columns 2 and 3 effect this separation in two different ways. The model in column 2 retains the multiplicative specification of mean income and X while the variances enter additively. These estimates indicate the mean income of black households and the variance of incomes of white household incomes to be significant determinants of relative ownership rates.[c] Greater variation of incomes around the mean for white households decreases the differences between races, while the effect of greater variation in black household income serves to increase the difference. In both cases the result stems from reduction in the rate of ownership of those in the lower income levels being greater than the increase in the rate of ownership at the higher

---

[c]The value of the coefficients expected in the model in column 2 on the basis of the coefficient in column 1 and the mean value of the complimentary interactive variable were compared with the actual coefficients in column 2. This exercise revealed that the greatest errors in using the coefficient in column 1 to predict the effect of all the variables included in the independent variable in column 1 would have been for the variance in white incomes. The effect of a change in X_b/Y_b, on the other hand, would have been predicted very accurately. The effects of variance in incomes of blacks and X_w/Y_w would have been substantially in error also.

income levels which occur with an incremental increase in the variance of incomes.

The model in the third column specifies all three components of the independent variable in (6.3a) to enter additively. In this instance the level of income and X_b are both significant for black households but not for whites. The only income term which is significant for white households is the variance of incomes. The greater responsiveness of blacks to even equivalent prices within the same market was anticipated. Because the non-income-compensated price elasticity of demand for necessities is greater for the poor, black ownership rates would be more than proportionately reduced. For the included cities, though, X_b on average was 134 percent of X_w.[d] The coefficients in column 3, then, reflect the combination of higher prices to blacks and the effect a sizable reduction in the homeownership rate of black households.

Of central importance, though, is the comparative effect of an increment to the income of blacks, holding the variance fixed, versus the effect of a decrease in the price of owner-occupied housing to blacks. Based on the results in column 3, the elasticity of the log of the rate of ownership of blacks relative to whites with respect to Y_b and X_b evaluated at the means are 0.113 and 0.071, respectively. The effect of a percentage change in Y_b on the relative rate of ownership, then, is about one and half times that of a reduction in the price of owner-occupied housing to blacks as measured by X_b. Evaluation of the effect of a percentage change in Y_b/Y_w on relative ownership ratio from the model in column 5 of Table 6-2 (which uses a reciprocal rather than s-shaped specification of the income-tenure relation[e]) indicates a mean elasticity of about 1.6—an

---

[d]The means of some of important phenomena are as follows:

Variable	Mean Value	
	White Households	Black Households
Real income	12847	8111
Standard deviation of mean income	7484	5631
X_j	12694	17036
Probability of homeownership	.636	.424

[e]The relationship between the probability of ownership and income for a household is, as indicated, s-shaped, which can be approximated for linear analysis by a reciprocal-logarithmic transformation. A less exact approximation of this relationship can be obtained from a simple reciprocal transformation. Since the relationship between mean income and the coefficient of variation of income was found to be reciprocal, use of the coefficient of variation of income instead of simply the mean of income in the aggregate tenure probability-income relation has the effect of transforming the reciprocal probability-income relation into a linear one and at the same time introduces the distribution as well as the mean of income into the function. This formulation is clearly less rigorous than that derived in the text, but it seems to offer a useful approximation. Inclusion of this model also serves to emphasize the sensitivity of some of the results to the functional specification of the model.

Table 6-2
Estimated Regression Models of Relative Black Homeownership Rates[a]

Variable	(1)	(2)	(3)	(4)	Variable	(5)	(6)
	Dependent variable: $\ln\,[(P(b)/P(w))\,*1000.]$					Dependent variable: $P(b)/P(w)$	
Constant	6.78 (120)	5.88 (9.65)	4.88 (6.54)	7.40 (20.2)	Constant	1.004 (5.77)	.286 (.62)
$\dfrac{X_b}{Y_b}e^{(.5)\sigma_b^2} - \dfrac{X_w}{Y_w}e^{(.5)\sigma_w^2}$	.557 (5.94)				Y_b/Y_w	1.74 (2.98)	
X_b/Y_b		−.238 (5.99)	−.164 (1.45)		$\dfrac{\text{std. dev. } Y_b}{\text{std. dev. } Y_w}$	−1.64 (3.12)	
X_w/Y_w		.120 (1.01)			X_b/X_w	−.146 (3.12)	
$e^{(.5)\sigma_b^2}$		−.726 (.75)			Y_b		.00019 (3.05)
$e^{(.5)\sigma_w^2}$		3.42 (3.76)	4.43 (4.25)		Y_w		−.00019 (3.53)
Y_b			.00009 (2.48)		std. dev. Y_b		−.00027 (2.66)
Y_w			.00002 (.83)		std. dev. Y_w		.00025 (2.91)
X_b			−.00003 (5.70)		X_b		−.00001 (4.51)
X_w			.000003 (.30)		X_w		$-2.3*10^{-6}$ (.37)

Y_b/Y_w				.590 (1.24)		
$e^{(.5)\sigma_b^2}/e^{(.5)\sigma_w^2}$				−.792 (2.80)		
X_b/X_w				−.269· (4.12)		
$\bar{R}^2$	.550	.657	.670	.497	.547	.665
F	35.2	14.4	10.5	10.2	12.2	10.2

aStudent t-statistics are in parentheses beneath the coefficients.

extremely powerful effect. In this specification, the mean elasticity of Y_b/Y_w is about five times as great as that of X_b/X_w. No matter which specification is used, however, the point is the same: increasing black incomes would be more effective in increasing the relative homeownership rate of blacks than similar decreases in the higher prices which blacks face presumably resultant from discriminatory practices.

Also of empirical interest are the determinants of $X_b - X_w$. The mean difference between X_b and X_w is about \$4,300, which is significant at the 1 percent level. For only one of the included cities (Austin) is the difference negative, and for ten cities the difference is zero. The average difference for the remaining eighteen cities, then, is about \$13,000.

As indicated in development of the aggregate model, the difference in X's is expected to be a function of the size of the housing market, the characteristics of the housing stock, the characteristics of the households, and the effects of racial discrimination. The models in the first three columns of Table 6-3 provide some evidence on this issue.[f] Since a positive difference in $X_b - X_w$ is associated with a relatively higher price (or greater difficulty) of homeownership to black households, a negative effect (sign) of an independent variable indicates an increase in the variable will lower the price to blacks. According to the estimates larger SMSAs and those with a relatively higher percentage of the housing built before 1940 have relatively higher prices of black homeownership. Also there is some tendency for a high proportion of single-unit structures to reduce the price premium to blacks. Market size presumably reflects, in part, higher prices per unit of housing in general in the area due to greater land costs,[7] and the reason for the greater responsiveness of blacks to higher prices (which produces a higher X_b) has already been noted. The positive sign of the variable for the fraction of stock built before 1940 was not anticipated; the variable may be correlated with housing located in the older, more centralized parts of the cities which appears in general to be less desirable for owner-occupancy due to the poor quality of many public services, especially schools, available there.[8]

The single most remarkable aspect of the findings, though, is the consistent lack of significance of measures of residential racial segregation or supply restrictions (SNGUOWN) on the relative price of owner-occupancy to black households. Apparently, discrimination against blacks being homeowners is quite subtle and bears little relation to the comparatively obvious residential segregation in any given city.

---

[f]The family type variables outlined in the previous section were insignificant even for the non-husband-wife family types. This insignificance appears to be attributable to the relatively small degree of variation in these variables across sample cities. Also, since Table 6-3 could present only a few of the models estimated, those estimates including (P_h/P_t) are not shown; it was insignificant to explaining $X_b - X_w$. It was included as a possible replacement for the housing stock and market size variables, but apparently the individual attributes of the stock are more important in determining $X_j - X_w$ than a measure of overall price variation.

Estimated Regression Models for $(X_b - X_w)$ and Reduced Form Models of Relative Ownership Rates of Blacks[a]

Independent Variables	Dependent Variable						
	$X_b - X_w$			$1n[P(b)/P(w)]$ *1000.		$P(b)/P(w)$	
	(1)	(2)	(3)	(4)	(5)	(6)	(7)
Constant	5992 (.67)	8452 (.86)	-5326 (.30)	5.60 (12.0)	6.22 (8.58)	.687 (1.22)	.729 (1.23)
Percent of units in single units structures	-152.4 (1.36)	-161.3 (1.39)	-70.9 (.46)	.015 (4.00)	.011 (2.14)	.0084 (3.80)	.0073 (2.35)
Percent of units built 1939 or earlier	181.7 (2.67)	181.8 (2.64)	128.9 (1.44)	-.007 (2.63)	-.005 (1.62)	-.0022 (1.46)	-.0019 (1.09)
No. of housing units in market	.0022 (1.45)	.0022 (1.48)	.0028 (1.72)	$4.9*10^{-8}$ (.90)	$3.8*10^{-8}$ (.71)	$2.3*10^{-8}$ (.74)	$1.5*10^{-8}$ (.46)
NWT	1961 (.47)			.092 (.51)		-.043 (.43)	
GS/N		-923.5 (.33)					
SNGUOWN			.8921 (.92)		-.359 (1.08)		-.098 (.49)
Coefficient of variation of income of whites						.017 (2.50)	.017 (2.81)
Coefficient of variation of incomes of blacks						-.021 (2.93)	-.020 (2.66)
Y_b/Y_w				1.26 (2.52)	.995 (2.11)		
$(1/2)\sigma_b^2/(1/2)\sigma_w^2$				-.681 (1.98)	-.499 (1.77)		
$\bar{R}^2$	.433	.431	.427	.600	.616	.631	.632
F	6.35	6.29	5.17	8.00	8.47	8.98	9.01

[a]Student t-statistics are in parentheses beneath the coefficients.

The final four columns of Table 6-3 present reduced-form estimates of the determinants of the relative ownership rate of blacks. In these models the income variables have been condensed somewhat to conserve degrees of freedom. They are similar to prior estimates in three important respects; (1) the level and dispersion of incomes remain significant determinants, (2) measures of residential segregation and supply restrictions to blacks are insignificant, and (3) the degree of explained variance of the dependent variable in the reduced-form is about the same as in the models given in Table 6-2. One important difference can be noted, however. The most statistically significant variable in these models is the percentage of units in single-unit structures. In the models in columns 6 and 7 it has an elasticity at the mean of around 0.7, compared with similar elasticities of the coefficient of the variation of incomes of black and white households of -2.27 and 1.66, respectively.

The strength of the effects of the market characteristics compared to those of specific segregation effects suggests that the overall availability of housing which is desirable for owner-occupancy may be more important than discrimination as reflected in residential segregation. In fact it may be that a shortage of housing especially suited for owner-occupancy produces two reinforcing effects which work to the detriment of blacks. First, the shortage has the effect of bidding the price per unit of these dwellings up, a process which, as noted above, more than proportionately discourages black demand. Second, in a relatively tight market those who wish to practice discrimination will be able to do so at small cost to themselves since they will be able to sell or rent to whom they please with short vacancy periods.

Thus while on balance it is possible to conclude that the relative rate of black homeownership is reduced by the comparatively higher prices for owner-occupied housing which blacks face, it has not been possible to associate these higher prices with any obvious evidence of possible discrimination such as residential segregation. There is some suggestion, however, that overall market conditions may contribute to the ability of those in the market to discriminate. Still, though, the substantially greater effect of an increment to black incomes on the relative ownership rate of blacks compared with the effect of a reduction in price should be recalled to place the role of discrimination in a proper context.

Further Policy Discussion

The analysis of this and earlier chapters has established lower rates of homeownership of black households relative to white households at every income level and indicates that even at the highest levels of income the ownership rate of whites to be about 10 percent above those of black households. The primary policy implication of the formal econometric analysis is of a substantial comparative efficacy of increasing the incomes of black households versus decreasing the higher price of owner-occupancy which blacks face.

This section goes behind the definitions of incomes and the "price" of owner-occupancy of black households used in the econometric analysis to discuss more fully the causes of the differences in ownership rates and the implications of the broad policy prescription already set out. The basic goal is to amplify the policy directives and to make their application more concrete.

The main limitation of the income data used in the analysis of this and the prior chapter is that it is for the single calendar year, 1969. It differs, then, from the concept of permanent income used in the analysis of Chapter 4, and this can have important implications for the estimates and policy statements for several reasons. To begin, since 1969 was a comparatively good year for the national economy, the transitory components of the incomes of most households would be positive. However, since the employment and labor force participation rates of urban blacks, especially men, are more cyclically sensitive than their white counterparts, the transitory component is probably higher for blacks than for whites,[9] and this may cause our estimate of the difference in ownership rates to be overstated. An adjustment for this factor would certainly not eliminate the differences in homeownership rates. However, the difference between permanent and current incomes and the composition of family incomes offers some genuine insights into what may be happening.

The aspect of the composition of income of particular interest in this analysis is the importance of the earnings of wives for total incomes of husband-wife families, the group which constitutes about two-thirds of all black owner-occupant households (see Table 2-1). The tabulations on the number of earners and median incomes of black and white husband-wife families presented in Table 6-4 confirm the higher incidence of working wives among blacks. Not shown in the table, though, is the fact that the earnings of working black women are also more important to total family incomes than are the earnings of white wives in husband-wife households; black wives account for about one-third of total income compared with one-quarter for white wives' earnings.[10]

Table 6-4
Distribution of Husband-Wife Families and Median Family Income by Earnings Status of Husband and Wife by Race

	Whites Earner			Blacks Earner		
	All	Husband Only	Husband and Wife	All	Husband Only	Husband and Wife
Proportion of all husband-wife families	1.0	.34	.44	1.0	.25	.55
Median income ($000)	11.2	9.9	13.0	8.2	6.7	10.4

Source: Tables 65 and 6y of U.S. Bureau of the Census, *Current Population Reports*, Series P-60, No. 85 (Washington, D.C.: U.S. Government Printing Office, 1972).

The evidence, in short, points to black men having greater instability in their earnings over time and to black wives contributing a greater share to total family income than is the case for whites. The effect of these factors is to make black households less preferred as a group for mortgage loans. The practice of discounting the earnings of wives by savings institutions in judging the fitness of a mortgage applicant has apparently been widespread.[11] Furthermore, the Federal Housing Administration's guidelines for insuring loans until the late 1960s included both the discounting of wives earnings and a very careful policy regarding the area in which the mortgage property was located. These various factors have combined to make homeownership significantly more difficult for black households.

This seems to be confirmed by Duran Bell's analysis of the determinants of the level of total debt and short-term debt of those black and white families in which both the husband and wife worked full time. At the margin $100 of additional earnings of black men are associated with $6.75 additional short-term debt compared with $8.45 for white men; for total debt, however, the same $100 increases black debt by $20, only half of the increase for whites. In the same analysis earnings of black wives were found to contribute significantly to debt bearing, while white wives do not—presumably reflecting the greater importance of black wives' earnings to family income.[12]

Two types of policy interventions suggest themselves on the basis of this reasoning, both of which are being pursued through federal policies, however imperfectly. The first is the entire set of macroeconomic policies aimed at keeping the economy on a steady upward trend to reduce this cause of employment instability. Another aspect of the same policy is to increase the skills of the blacks and/or upgrade the degree of satisfaction derived from the jobs available to workers with their qualifications. The economic downturn of the first half of the 1970s and the problems of the "war on poverty" speak forcefully to the national frustrations in both of these areas.

The second area for policy initiatives is in the realm of changing the rules of thumb employed by the mortgage banking industry. The Housing Act of 1968 required the Federal Housing Administration to move in this direction; and, after some severe problems from precipitous actions, the congressional directives are producing more favorable results.[13] Also passed in 1968, the Federal Fair Housing Law prohibits discrimination against minorities in obtaining mortgage financing. On balance, it appears progress is being made, especially in making more sensible judgments about neighborhood quality and in eliminating the discounting of women's earnings. Still much more vigorous action and greater use of federal guarantees to demonstrate the soundness of these loans would be desirable.

In the last section it was noted that the average value of X_j for black households was 34 percent greater than that for white households. The prior discussion suggests some of this difference is due to the composition and stability of the incomes of black families and the practices of mortgage bankers. Another source of a higher price of owner-occupancy to blacks, strongly supported by Kain and Quigley, is the combination of a housing stock poorly suited for homeownership in black residential enclaves of many metropolitan areas and the difficulty of obtaining housing outside of the segregated areas.[g] The focus in our discussion will be the cost of obtaining owner-occupant housing outside the dominantly black area.

There are two distinct factors which can raise the cost of non-enclave housing to blacks: (a) the cost of obtaining information and (b) payment of a premium to obtain housing in a dominantly white area. The costs of information can be high because of the hesitancy of white realtors to show housing in white areas to blacks and because of the difficulty black realtors have in obtaining information on listings in white neighborhoods. John Yinger has described the reasons for the hesitancy of white brokers, emphasizing the sensitivity of brokers to doing anything which would reduce the number of client referrals and, more importantly, property listings with them.[14] Yinger also provides a number of examples of the way in which white brokers can discourage potential black buyers while staying within the letter of the law. It might be noted that the motivation of white brokers is simply profit from their own transactions; no racial dislike or profiting from properties in black areas need enter. At the same time black brokers find it difficult to provide the necessary services because of difficulties in obtaining membership in local multiple-listing services. J.T. Darden recounts the problems of a black real estate broker in obtaining membership in one of Pittsburgh's principal multi-list service; the broker obtained membership only through litigation.[15] The motivation for exclusion on the part of the multi-list services is more difficult to fathom, since the cost of reduced referrals, etc., to the individual broker members should be small. One feasible explanation is that the white broker will be held responsible for the sale to a black family by a black broker of a property initially listed with the white broker; this explanation, however, seems contrived.

The argument that blacks are charged higher prices for homes in white neighborhoods than white households is less convincing than the information costs argument. For this phenomena to occur on a widespread basis would require white sellers to nearly universally act in this manner. Under extremely tight market conditions such behavior might be approximated, but under normal conditions the cost of passing up offers on the dwelling at its "market price" would move whites to reassess their indulging in discrimination. Also other whites would find it profitable to buy previously white-owned properties and resell them to blacks, especially in areas on the brink of racial transition.[16]

Given the above facts, the main policy suggestion is for an increase in the

___

[g]It is clear that the availability of suitable housing within the black enclave is not sufficient to produce equality in homeownership rates between the races. The experience of Pittsburgh in this regard, as outlined in Chapter 4, demonstrates this point extremely well.

information to blacks on the homes available for purchase throughout a metropolitan area. One thrust at the federal level would be encouragement of membership of qualified black real estate agents with local real estate boards affiliated with the National Association of Real Estate Boards, since membership is frequently a prerequisite to obtaining entry to other realty organizations including multi-list services. Reducing the costs of obtaining membership in local multi-list firms should also be pushed, perhaps by basing the fees on use rather than membership. Even with national government support, though, it is likely that local litigation will be required, which means the flow of information can be expected to increase at a painfully slow rate.

7

Housing Allowances, Inflation, and Homeownership Rates

As demonstrated in the preceding chapters, there are an enormous number of factors which can affect the rate at which households choose to own their homes. The size and composition of households, the distribution of households in the life cycle, the growth and distribution of aggregate income among households, the prices of factors used to produce housing services which affect alterations in the size and type of dwellings in the housing stock, the spatial arrangement of the stock within urban areas, and household tastes and preferences come quickly to mind in an enumeration of these factors. In principle, the models which have been estimated in this volume could be employed in analysis of the effects on the frequency of homeownership of changes in these factors which come about through the normal course of events or through government intervention, either direct action or indirectly through the creation of incentives.

The purpose of this chapter is to illustrate this type of analysis for two topics of interest in their own right. Specifically, the effects on the rate of household homeownership of a national housing allowance program and of an increase in the price of owner-occupied housing relative to rental housing are studied. Housing allowances are a proposed system of cash transfers to needy households from the federal government earmarked in some manner for expenditure on housing. Price increases, on the other hand, result from the interaction of market forces; but, judging from the expressions in the popular press, they are nevertheless of widespread interest. Finally, since the models estimated in the prior chapters are for urban households, the analyses in this chapter likewise only apply to metropolitan areas.

Housing Allowances and Homeownership

In the United States it has been traditional for aid in the area of housing to take the form of reducing the cost of housing to the needy; in other words, the strategies have affected the supply of housing to this group, not their demand for housing.[1] At an extreme is the actual provision of housing by the federal government through the public housing program in which housing cost is determined by the household's income, adjusted for family size. Similarly, the major federal interventions in the housing market of the late 1960s used the device of lowering housing costs to the needy by subsidizing the interest rates paid by both developers and individual homeowners. "Operation Breakthrough," the program to achieve substantial reductions in the cost of newly constructed units, is another example of the attempt to reduce the gap between the cost of standard quality housing and the housing which low income households can afford when they spend 25 to 30 percent of their incomes on housing.

Early in the seventies, the executive branch of the federal government began moving away from these supply-side interventions. In part there was discouragement with the performance of the interest-subsidy and other programs, in part there was a growing recognition of the fact that most of the lowest income households were not participating in these programs,[2] and in part the Nixon Administration had a preference for programs which minimally disturb the functioning of the private housing market. The response to these several different forces was the initiation of an intense study of demand-side programs, programs designed to increase the demand for housing services by poor households sufficiently to achieve the goal of standard housing for all households.

These programs are generally referred to as housing allowances. A housing allowance is a general system of cash grants to low-income households based on some indication of housing need and intended to be spent largely on housing.[3] In fact, housing allowances have two potentially conflicting goals: (a) relief of poverty and (b) improvement of the quality of housing consumed by low-income households. The relative weight which is placed on each of these objectives produces actual programs with sharply differing characteristics. For example, emphasis on the housing quality goal would result in more checks being built in to assure the cash grant being spent on increased housing services. Such requirements, though, would likely reduce the rate of participation in the program which could introduce equity problems and obstruct achievement of the poverty-reduction goal. If relief of poverty were emphasized, there would be much less concern with expenditure patterns; and the main advantage of a housing allowance compared to a direct cash assistance plan would be political viability.

This section analyzes the effects, which would occur over a period as long as a decade, on the rate of homeownership of all households eligible nationally for one specific type of housing allowance program. The following paragraphs will first describe the program used for the analysis in general terms. Then the assumptions and procedures used in making the computations are outlined, and finally the changes in the homeownership rates are discussed. In this analysis a number of difficult operational problems regarding the inclusion of owner-occupant as well as renter households in an allowance program are ignored.[4] The general results presented are based on the assumption that those administrative difficulties can be overcome.

The housing plan utilized here contains components of what have been variously termed "housing-gap" or "minimum-housing-condition" plans. Under the plan the household must live in a unit which meets minimum standards in order to participate in the program, and it receives an income supplement based on the difference between the cost of such housing and the amount it can afford reasonably to spend on housing. The standards could be defined either in terms of physical attributes—plumbing, heating, structural soundness—or in terms of rents per month for standard housing in a local market. The magnitude of the income supplement declines as household income rises until it reaches zero at some income cutoff.[5] The formula determining the subsidy (S) is $S = C - bY$, where C is the maximum supplement payable, i.e., the payment to households with no income; Y is the income of the household, possibly adjusted for family size; and b is the tax rate or the rate at which the supplement is reduced as income rises, usually 0.2 or 0.25 in the plans under wide discussion. The income level at which the supplement reaches zero is C/b. Frequently C is defined so as to coincide with the cost of housing just meeting the minimal housing standards; this definition is used in the computations presented below. When defined in this way S is the dollar value of the "gap" between standard housing cost (C) and the expenditures the household can reasonably afford (bY). Note, though, that there is no necessity for this coincidence. The program might be structured for the cost of the minimal standard to exceed C; in this instance the lowest income participating households would frequently have to spend in excess of 30 percent of their income on housing. This would likely mean a reduction in expenditures on other items. Alternatively, setting C at a high level relative to the cost of minimal quantity would encourage participation and allow most households to have more money to spend on other things.

In analyzing the effects of the implementation of a housing allowance program on the homeownership patterns of participating households, there are five related aspects of the program itself or its consequences which must be confronted: (1) the stringency of the minimal consumption requirements and their relation to the size of the income supplement; (2) the extent to which the income supplements are converted into housing expenditures, i.e., the size of the earmarking ratio;[a] (3) the participation rate among households nominally eligible for the program; (4) the size of the program, i.e., the fraction of all households which are eligible; and (5) the extent to which the increase in income is dissipated in higher housing prices which results from the infusion of the allowance-induced housing demand. The treatment of these five aspects are discussed in turn below. The general objective, though, is fairly simple, namely, to convert the increased housing expenditures induced by the allowance program into an equivalent increase in income as if there had been no features of the program causing greater expenditures on housing and in turn to use the revised income data with the tenure choice models estimated in Chapter 5 to estimate changes on homeownership rates.

The five aspects of the allowance program enumerated in the last paragraph

---

[a]The earmarking ratio is the ratio of the change in housing expenditures of the household to the cash supplement received by the household.

are clearly interrelated, and one cannot address them until a specific allowance program is chosen. The program selected is one in which, on a national basis, 22 percent of all households would be eligible for some payment. This is a large-scale national program of the type under study by the Department of Housing and Urban Development. Also as in the prototype, a tax rate of 0.2 is used. With the maximum participant income, which is also the income cutoff, determined by the size of the program and the tax rate given, the value of maximum payment is also determined ($C = bY$, with Y defined at the income cutoff). Hence under a gap program, as eligibility and the cutoff are increased, the depth of the subsidy also rises. As a consequence the lowest income households will receive substantial income supplements with a major national program. The other dominant characteristic of the program concerns the minimum housing consumption required for program participation. As noted above, the cost of the minimum standard dwelling has been assumed to be approximately equal to the maximum subsidy payment (C). From analysis cited below, it is known that this corresponds to a modestly stringent consumption requirement.

In making assumptions regarding participation rates, earmarking, and effects on the price of housing services advantage has been taken of the extensive analysis of housing allowance programs which have been done using the Urban Institute housing market simulation model. Since this model predicts the effects of policies on the housing consumption and location of households in a given metropolitan area over a ten-year period, it corresponds to the long-run framework adopted for the present analysis. These analyses strongly indicate that effects of housing allowances depend critically on the conditions prevailing in local housing markets, such as the quality distribution of the local stock, the growth in the number of households over the period and their distribution with respect to income, and the price elasticity of supply of the stock of housing present at the beginning of the period.[6] The parameter values used here are rough averages over varying market conditions.

The results of these simulations suggest that, on average, about 60 percent of the income supplements received by participating households will be devoted to purchasing more housing services. Further, on economic grounds about 90 percent of the eligible households will participate.[b] The most volatile aspect of the allowance simulations is the effect of the program on the price of housing services consumed by eligible households. A reasonable rate of inflation in the price per unit of housing services over the decade in which the program is implemented seems to be about 10 percent.

Given the assumptions of the previous paragraph the computation of the level

---

[b]That is, households determine if they would be better off in economic terms to participate in the program. Hence the participation rate does not include refusals based on poor information, the stigma associated with accepting "charity," etc. However, since the simulations apply to a ten-year period over which most of these barriers to participation would presumably be removed, use of the full 90 percent seems justified.

of *housing income*, i.e., the increase in income required to produce the observed increase in housing expenditures in the absence of minimum consumption requirements, is reasonably straightforward. The increase in expenditures is calculated as 60 percent of the income supplement received, and this is converted into a percentage change in expenditures.[7] The estimate of housing income was then made by assuming an income elasticity of demand for housing of service of 1.0, i.e., each percentage increase in expenditures would have required a 1 percent increase in income.[8] These computations were made separately for the households in each income interval for which the Census publishes the requisite information. The rates of homeownership under the program were calculated, then, by substituting the higher income figures the tenure-choice model estimated in Chapter 5 for all households combined.[c]

Finally, since the results of simulating housing allowance programs indicate the effects on the housing consumption of ineligible households to be negligible, the homeownership rates of these households are assumed to be unaffected by the program.[d] The results of the computations just described are summarized in Table 7-1. Column 3 shows the percentage increase in housing expenditures for households eligible for the program. For the lowest (current) income households, the change is over a third of the base; note, though, that a portion of this increase goes for higher housing prices. The final two columns in the table indicate the effects on the aggregate homeownership rates by income class. For the lowest income class about 4 percent of all households are estimated to switch from rental to owner tenure.[e] The portion switching decreases as income rises because of the reduction in the amount of the subsidy received. The highest income but still program-eligible households actually suffer a slight decline in ownership rates. This result is caused by the reduction of the real incomes of these households which is produced by the combination of their receiving only small housing allowance payments but experiencing the full force of the increase in the price of housing services. For lower income households the subsidy

---

[c]It had originally been planned to prepare estimates for the individual household types analyzed in Chapters 4 and 5. The published Census data are not, however, sufficiently detailed for this purpose. Also, for clarity, the model used is the final regression model given in Table D-2. In using this model, the value of X_i, the income of "indifference" which reflects the cost of housing and owneroccupancy in the tenure choice models, was increased by 10 percent to account for the rise in the price of housing caused by implementation of the allowance program.

[d]In the simulations, those households pay taxes of about 1 percent of their incomes, after exemptions, to finance the program, and it is for this reason and due to inflation that changes in their housing consumption would be anticipated.

[e]It might be recalled from Chapter 5 that the predictive ability of the model being used for these computations is weakest for the lowest income households. The model underpredicts the rate of homeownership in this range; it is not clear, however, that it will underestimate increments to homeownership from increased income, given the fact that it is based on current rather than permanent income. The increments shown in the table are based on the model estimated in Chapter 5; the base year rates are the actual range from the Census of Housing.

Table 7-1
Estimated Effects on Homeownership of a Housing Allowance Program

Income Interval	Number of Households[b] (000's)	Base Mean Monthly Housing Expenditures[b]	Percent Change in Housing Expenditures of Allowance Program Participants	Homeownership Rate		Change in the Number of Homeowners from Allowance Program (000's)
				Base	Change With Allowance Program	
Under $2,000	4,497	$104	34.9	.404	.044	197
2,000-2,999	2,313	106	20.0	.422	.024	55
3,000-3,999	2,243	112	10.1	.423	.002	4
4,000-4,999	2,216	116	.1	.429	-.019	-42
5,000-5,999	2,392	120	a	.434	a	a
6,000-6,999	2,517	124	a	.461	a	a
7,000-9,999	8,159	135	a	.564	a	a
10,000-14,999	10,664	162	a	.701	a	a
15,000-24,999	6,796	209	a	.793	a	a
Over 24,999	2,061	310	a	.836	a	a

[a]Households ineligible for allowance.
[b]Base is 1970; base data from U.S. Bureau of the Census, *Metropolitan Housing Characteristics*, Report HC(2)-1, United States and Regions (Washington, D.C.: U.S. Government Printing Office, 1972).

payments exceed the price-caused income reductions, and higher income households generally escape the inflation while receiving no subsidy.

On balance the effects of a national housing allowance program on the rate of homeownership in urban areas, under the assumptions made above, would likely be quite modest. About 2 percent of the eligible households or roughly some 210,000 households could on net shift from rental to owner-occupant status. These results, though, ignore any possible additional shifts which might be caused by active encouragement of homeownership in the program. Such encouragement might range from counseling services to deeper subsidies for households shifting tenure, and could have considerable additional effects beyond those which have been estimated.

Homeownership Effects of the
Rising Price of Owner-Occupancy

One hears public officials and politicians remarking with great frequency that owner-occupied housing is becoming beyond the economic grasp of an increasing proportion of households. Unfortunately this statement is seldom refined by the speaker, so that the earlier period with which current times are being implicitly compared is left undefined, as is the measure of costs or prices of owner-occupied housing being used. All too often one has the feeling such statements are based on smatterings of data which themselves may be badly misleading.

This section has two general objectives. The first is simply to introduce a greater degree of precision into the discussion of trends in the cost of homeownership by (a) making some conceptual distinctions between short-run and long-run effects of changes in factor prices on the price of housing per unit of service and (b) briefly examining the commonly reported statistics in view of these distinctions. Using this material and estimates from Chapter 5 as inputs, the consequences of increases in the price per unit of owner-occupied housing relative to rental housing over the 1967-1973 period are analyzed. More specifically the near-term or contemporaneous effects of higher prices on the rate of homeownership of households making their first home purchase are studied, and then the effects of a sustained change in the prices of factors used in producing housing and hence in the price per unit of services between the two tenure forms over a longer period, say ten to fifteen years, are projected.

To use the estimated models in Chapter 5 for this analysis requires some strong assumptions; effectively conditions have to remain as they were in 1970, i.e., the preferences of households for owner-occupancy and the very broad characteristics of the stock of dwellings must remain unaltered. These are, of course, stringent assumptions; and since adjustments have and will continue to take place, the estimated effects presented below are best treated as the upper bound to the actual shifts in tenure which would occur in response to the price changes. Finally, although these estimates are based on the experience of a particular period, the differential short-run and long-run consequence of the shifts in prices are emphasized as the general results will likely hold for other periods.

For a shift in tenure to occur, holding preferences and household composition constant requires the price per unit of housing services to owner-occupants to change relative to that for rental services.[f] One can easily imagine conditions under which these two prices could not diverge. This would be exactly the situation if the stock of housing were perfectly divisible and mobile or, equivalently, if the entire stock were replaced annually or if the demand for tenure were infinitely price elastic. Such possibilities are, though, sharply at variance with the real world; in fact the two attributes of housing which distinguish it from other goods are the combination of durability and the association of a particular set of neighborhood conditions with the structure itself. Further, as emphasized in the conceptual discussion of Chapters 3 and 4, households exhibit strong preferences for each tenure mode, and these are sufficient to yield the assumption of infinite price elasticity clearly inoperable.[9] In this same vein, the statistics on the type of dwelling inhabited by homeowners indicate that there has traditionally been a joint demand for the single-unit structure and owner-occupancy.

The consequences of the durability of the stock and the characteristics of neighborhoods and the less than perfectly elastic demands have their effects over time on the price per unit of service of housing. Assume that when a city was initially founded, the price per unit of all inputs for the construction of housing—land, labor, capital, etc.—were the same and that all of the factors were in plentiful supply. All housing would cost the same per unit of service, and the cost of housing would differ only by virtue of the quantity of services a housing bundle contained; finally, the quantity of services demanded and their mix— large or small lot, small or big structure—would depend on the demand of the initial purchaser. As time progresses if one factor used relatively intensively in the construction of owner-occupied housing, say land, rises in price relative to other inputs, the price per unit of housing services from those dwellings already in the stock will likewise rise. The price per unit of service of new structures built for owner-occupants could be the same or lower as that of the older dwellings depending on whether the new units economized on land in producing the same quantity of services.[g]

Something quite similar to our hypothetical scenario has actually been occurring in the United States. The typical household's definition of its own home, the single-family detached dwelling, has remained remarkably stable in the face of shifts in the relative prices of factors needed for both construction

---

[f]Housing services are defined here as they were at the beginning of Chapter 3.

[g]Services are on a flow basis, so the expected life of the structure, i.e., the stock of services, does not enter into the argument.

and operation. It is important to note, though, that there is no divergence in the price of the same dwelling by tenure form. There is, rather, a divergence in the composition of inputs used to produce the types of dwellings in which owner-occupants and renters prefer to live; and the result is a divergence in the average price per unit of housing services between the two tenure forms. If the distributions of preferences and demands for housing bundles of renters and owner-occupants were identical, there would be no divergence in prices.

From the foregoing it is clear that the price index one selects to determine the course of the relative price per unit of owner-occupied housing depends on the question one wants to address. If the focus is on the price per unit of the traditional owner-occupied dwelling, one should select some such standard unit and essentially observe the average price of services from such dwellings over time. If, on the other hand, the focus is on the price paid by all owner-occupants then the average price per unit of services from all owner-occupied properties should be used. The difference between the two measures is that the latter allows for adjustments in the demand and supply of dwellings for homeowners in response to price signals, adjustments both in the quantity of services and in the factor input composition of these services. As stated at the beginning of this section, because the estimated tenure choice models do not allow for this kind of adjustment, the first type of price change measure is relevant for our analysis; again note the overstatement in the effects on tenure choice which this embodies.

The statistics generally relied upon to measure the change in the price of housing relative to other goods and income and the change in price of housing by tenure form are components of the Consumer Price Index (CPI) compiled and published by the U.S. Bureau of Labor Statistics (BLS). Unfortunately both the rent index and the cost of homeownership index are likely subject to significant biases which limits their usefulness for the present computations.[10]

The homeownership cost index is the monthly cost of a dwelling and is composed of five separate categories: (1) mortgage-interest, (2) maintenance and repairs, (3) property taxes, (4) insurance, and (5) the purchase price of the home. In determining the changes in these components, the BLS has tried to hold the housing bundle constant by gathering information on dwellings of a fairly specific set of characteristics. However, since the dwellings sampled are only those recently purchased (but not necessarily newly constructed), the dwellings included in the sample vary from period to period which introduces some variability in the dwellings sampled. Sampling only recent sales also has the effect of substantially overstating the effect of recent trends in the purchase price of homes and mortgage interest rates on the average cost of owner-occupied housing. Since the weights of these two items constitute about 62 percent of the total homeowner index, the consequences of this procedure are formidable. In periods of rising trends in these factors, like the 1967-1973 period, this clearly biases the index upwards. Further, since once a household purchases a home it will on average enjoy the mean rate of capital appreciation and hence will have maintained its initial downpayment in real terms, the change in purchase price dominantly affects households purchasing their first homes. Changes in the other three components of the index apply to the stock of owner-occupants. In summary, the cost of homeownership index applies most directly to the cost of a traditional owner-occupied dwelling which is faced by those households purchasing their first home.

The rent index is similar to the homeownership cost index in that it too applies over time to units of the same characteristics. On the other hand, the rent index is calculated by comparing rent changes of the same apartment from period to period, which holds the dwelling characteristics much more rigidly fixed for rental than for owner-occupied units. In general, then, the rent index should be more reliable. However, the fact that the index is not adjusted for the aging of the apartments included in the sample leads some researchers to conclude that the index may be biased downward.[h] Another factor which may be distorting the index is the relative decline over time of central city neighborhoods in which rental units are concentrated; since rents include the amenities of the area, a reduction in neighborhood quality, which would not be sufficient in many cases to cause a dwelling to be dropped from the sample, would produce an overstatement of the decline in price. Overall the bias from depreciation is likely greater than that from neighborhood considerations so that the rental index may have the defect of being somewhat downwardly biased. It does, though, have the virtue of applying to the entire stock of rental housing.

The data in the CPI does provide some guidance for determining the extent of the rise in the relative price per unit of owner-occupied housing services faced by first time home purchasers. The data in Table 7-2 show that over the 1967-1973 period the homeowner index increase was nearly double that of the rent index. Making a generous 20 percent allowance for understatement in the renter index, the difference in the relative price change of owner-occupied services relative to rental services is computed to be 47 percent $(100.(47-29)/.5(47+29))$. This change must be converted into a shift in X_j, the "income of indifference" (changes in which mirror changes in the price of owner-occupied housing) defined in Chapter 5, in order to predict the reduction in homeownership rates which it produces. Since the short-term effect on first-time purchasers is the initial subject of the analysis, use of a shift in X_j by an amount equivalent to the price change would overstate the extent of the adjustment. In some housing markets before the price change, for example, the rate of homeownership may

---

[h]The problem arises when the depreciation of a dwelling results in a reduced flow of services from that dwelling while the BLS believes the services have not been reduced; assuming rents decline, the quantity decrease is reported as a price decrease. It should be noted that new units are added to the sample and older units dropped, but rent changes are also computed on a dwelling specific basis so that the above problem is not resolved by adding new units. Resolution would require inter-dwelling comparisons, which have the cost of reducing the extent of standardization in the service flow in the dwellings being compared.

Table 7-2

Percentage Changes in the Rent and Homeowner Cost Components of the Consumer Price Index, 1953-1973

	Period		
Component	1953-1973	1963-1973	1967-1973
Rent	55%	31%	24%
Homeownership	96	65	47

Source: From Table 1 in J.C. Weicher and J.C. Simonson, "Recent Trends in Housing Costs," *Journal of Economics and Business*, 1975, p. 177. Reprinted by permission.

have been constrained by a shortage in the supply of suitable structures. It is not possible to determine the short-term, relative price elasticity of X_j, so the effects on the homeownership rate of first purchasers have been computed separately under assumptions that 70 percent and 90 percent of the 47 percent relative price change is translated into shifts in X_j. "First purchasers" are defined as husband-wife families with heads under the age of thirty. This definition is obviously somewhat narrow, but it is adequate to illustrate the degree of shift in ownership rates which would occur.

The second issue to be addressed is the longer run consequence of a shift in relative prices of housing services by tenure. As argued earlier the extent of the change in prices depends on the changes in individual factor prices and the intensity of the use of specific factors in various types of dwellings. In the intermediate run, mortgage rates and insurance rates will become nearly equivalent for the average unit in both tenure forms. Land prices and labor costs may be the most important sources of price shifts between tenure forms since there are definite but different limits to the degree to which other factors can be substituted for them under each tenure form. For the present analysis, a 10 percent increase in the relative price of owner-occupied services is simply assumed, since hard data on these factors are extremely difficult to obtain. It is also assumed that in the long run the full increase in price is reflected in X_j.[i]

The basic estimates of the effects of the price increases just outlined on the rate of homeownership are shown for households of selected incomes in Table 7-3. Turning initially to the short-run effects on "first purchasers," the data in the top panel of the table indicate a sharp effect: for households with income of

[i]The models actually used in making these estimates are the cross-SMSA models described in Chapter 5 and reported in Appendix Table D-2; the models estimated with the arithmetic mean of homeownership rates for husband-wife households with head under age thirty and for all households combined are used. The base rates of homeownership were predicted using the mean value of X_j with the specified income level. As noted in Chapter 5 for the current low income households, especially of all household types combined, the predictions are biased upwards. These have not been adjusted in the results reported here as the biases do not materially effect the results.

Table 7-3
Effects of an Increase in the Price Per Unit of Services of Owner-Occupied Housing Relative to Rental Housing

A. Short-Term Effects on First Purchasers of 47 Percent Price Increase

Rates of Homeownership

Income Level	Base Case	With increase in price of owner-occupied housing services	
		70 Percent Adjustment in X_j	90 Percent Adjustment in X_j
$2,000	.030	.011	.011
4,000	.129	.077	.075
6,000	.199	.149	.148
8,000	.259	.204	.202
10,000	.301	.248	.246
14,000	.355	.310	.308
18,000	.389	.362	.360
22,000	.414	.379	.380
30,000	.444	.417	.416

B. Effects on the Stock of Owner-Occupants of 10 Percent Price Increase

Rates of Homeownership

Income Level	Base Case	With Price Increase
$2,000	.292	.262
4,000	.504	.477
6,000	.610	.582
8,000	.632	.612
10,000	.699	.684
14,000	.743	.732
18,000	.769	.760
22,000	.786	.779
30,000	.807	.801

$10,000 there is an 18 percent reduction in the homeownership rate; for lower income households the reductions are even greater over 40 percent at $6,000; and even for households with incomes of $20,000 the reduction is about 10 percent. By any standard these are sharp shifts in the rate of homeownership, and they are likely the changes which fuel the comments appearing in the popular press.

With the owner-occupants and landlords eventually facing the same level of factor prices over time, much of the short-run disparity in the price per unit of housing services under the two tenure forms vanishes. Panel B of the table shows the estimated effects on the aggregate rate of homeownership of a 10 percent rise in the relative price of owner-occupied services which is sustained for a decade or more. The effects are quite small: at the $6,000 income level, the homeownership rate is reduced by 4.6 percent, and at levels over $10,000 the change in the rate declines from 2 percent to less than 1 percent. Note that these estimates assume that the stock of housing remains unchanged, so that new units added to the stock would not economize on the relatively expensive input factors. Similarly, there is no allowance for the widespread presence of condominium or cooperatives. Hence the longer-term consequences of a shift in the price of factor inputs used relatively intensively in owner-occupied housing would appear to be quite modest. Indeed, the effects of increases in the price of all housing services relative to other goods and services, shifts in household preferences, or changes in the structure of households are likely to have much greater effects than changes in the prices of these factor inputs.

Appendixes

Appendix A:
Joint Determination of
Tenure Choice and Housing
Consumption Decisions of
Individual Households

The model formulated in Equation (4.1) in Chapter 4 is a fairly conventional statement of the tenure choice decision; and one which, when carefully estimated, should yield useful results. However, it was believed that use of a single equation model could lead to biased estimates. If tenure choice is jointly determined with other decisions, the specification in (4.1) would attribute some of the variance actually accounted for by the residual to the independent variables and thus lead to inconsistent estimates.

The decision to which the tenure decision is most closely related is that on the quantity of housing services demanded (directly and as a derived demand the magnitude of the stock in which to invest). Further, the magnitude of the federal tax subsidy depends on the tenure decision, the amount of housing services demanded, and the fraction of housing expenses which are deductible.

The demand for housing services by households has been greatly studied.[1] The typical formulation makes the quantity of services demanded a function of income and household characteristics and prices when different markets are being studied. One additional factor is the level of housing services demanded by the household's peer group, similar to the tenure probability of peers. The demand for services of household j of family type i, then, can be written as follows, using the notation defined in the section "Theoretical Framework" of Chapter 4:

$$Q_{ji} = c_0 + c_1 Y_{ji} + c_2 \text{pers}_{ji} + c_3 \text{fam}_{ji} + c_4 S_j \qquad (A.1)$$
$$+ c_5 T_{ji} + c_6 Q\text{Peer}_j + c_7 X_1$$

where:

Q_{ji} = the quantity of housing services demanded by household j of family type i

$Q\text{Peer}$ = the quantity of housing services demanded by household j's peer group

X_1 = summarizes other factors determining Q_{ji} omitted from the current formulation.

Finally, the federal subsidy which is hypothesized to affect both tenure choice and the quantity of services demanded,[a] can be stated to be a function of the level of permanent income and the value of housing services; the coefficients will implicitly reflect the rate at which potentially deductible expenses are actually deducted.

$$S_j = d_1 + d_2 Y_{ji} + d_3 Q_{ji} + d_4 T_{ji} \tag{A.2}$$

Note that by treating the tax subsidy as affecting the price of housing to the household rather than the household's income, it is not necessary to jointly determine income with the subsidy.

The three-equation system in which tenure choice, the demand for housing services, and the federal tax subsidy are jointly determined is as follows where an asterisk indicates a jointly determined variable.

$$T_{ji}^* = e_0 + e_1 \ln Y_{ji} + e_2 \text{pers}_{ji} + e_3 \text{fam}_{ji} + e_4 S_j^* \tag{A.3a}$$
$$+ e_5 \text{peer} + e_6 Q_{ji}^* + e_7 X_2$$

$$Q_{ji}^* = f_0 + f_1 Y_{ji} + f_2 \text{pers}_{ji} + f_3 \text{fam}_{ji} + f_4 T_j^* \tag{A.3b}$$
$$+ f_5 Q \text{peer} + f_6 X_1 + f_7 S_j$$

$$S_j^* = g_0 + g_1 Y_{ji} + g_2 Q_j^* + g_3 T_{ji}^* \tag{A.3c}$$

Estimated Models for White Households

Table A-1 presents a summary of the models for each household type in which tenure choice, housing expenditures, and the subsidy were treated as being

[a]The elasticities of the demand for housing services in which income has been adjusted for the federal tax advantages of homeownership were estimated by David Laidler for owners and renters separately. By keeping owners and renters separate he did not confront the problem of determining disposable family income (and housing expenditures) under the opposite tenure form for each household. As owners and renters must be combined in the sample for this study, treating the subsidy as a price effect was both more natural and a necessity. For details of Laidler's estimates, see his *Income Tax Incentives of Homeownership*, Ph.D. dissertation, University of Chicago, 1964.

The above formulation has omitted a fundamental aspect to the tenure decision—the investment in housing stock. A more complete model in which the investment and consumption decisions are jointly determined has been derived, but was not stated here because of the severe data limitations which prevent its estimation.

Table A-1
Two-Stage Least Squares Summary

| | Husband-Wife Families, Head: | | | | | | | |
| | Under Age 30 | | Age 30-44 Not dependent[a] | | Age 45-65 | | Over Age 65 Not dependent[a] | |
Independent Variables	T_{ji}	Q_{ji}	T_{ji}	Q_{ji}	T_{ji}	Q_{ji}	T_{ji}	Q_{ji}
Constant	1.09		−2.52 (9.21)	−98.0 (5.70)	.253 (2.12)	−13.6 (.69)	.626 (9.46)	−84.1 (.79)
Number of Persons					.069 (2.30)			26.5 (1.21)
Number of Persons^2					−.0059 (1.77)			
Current Income	.250 (2.98)				.0007 (1.82)		.0015 (1.66)	
Current Income^2					−3x10^{-6} (3.62)		−3.7x10^{-6} (1.99)	
Rate of ownership of Peer Group	.047 (.12)				.126 (.69)			
Moved into House 1967-70, 1 = Yes		31.3 (2.40)		38.4 (5.00)	−3.74 (9.34)	99.6 (6.37)	−9.21 (4.31)	−382. (1.30)
Calculated[b] tax subsidy: Q_{ij}/Y_{ij}	.268 (.27)	354. (1.70)	4.74 (9.62)	219. (4.42)	1.41 (3.05)	468.1 (5.23)		290. (1.41)
Calculated[b] Q_{ij}	.0013 (1.84)			−.002 (3.47)	.0012 (3.09)		.0063 (1.87)	
Calculated[b] T_{ij}		93.9 (2.79)		117.5 (6.12)		380.8 (7.90)		−.906 (1.26)
3-4 Persons in Household, 1 = Yes				.155 (2.87)				
5-6 Persons in Household, 1 = Yes				.319 (6.04)				
9+ Persons in Household, 1 = Yes				.375 (6.06)				
Permanent Income	.0045 (1.18)	.692 (5.46)	.0038 (10.4)	1.17 (14.4)		1.16 (18.9)		.096 (3.29)
Housing Expenditures of Peer Group		−.26 (1.10)		−2.54		−2.54 (7.25)		5.54 (1.34)
Permanent Income^2	−.00002 (1.42)		−.0001 (10.6)					

Table A-1 (cont.)

Independent Variables	Husband-Wife Families, Head:							
	Under Age 30		Age 30-44 Not dependent[a]		Age 45-65		Over Age 65 Not dependent[a]	
	T_{ji}	Q_{ji}	T_{ji}	Q_{ji}	T_{ji}	Q_{ji}	T_{ji}	Q_{ji}
$1n$ (Persons in Household)	.388 (4.65)							
$1n$ (Current Income)	.113 (2.73)							
Reduced Form, R^2	.151	.280	.237	.445	.123	.376	.092	.098

Independent Variables	Other Family Not dependent[a]		Primary Individual	
	T_{ji}	Q_{ji}	T_{ji}	Q_{ji}
Constant	.187 (.99)	−9.00 (.93)	−.012 (1.34)	13.2 (1.07)
Female Head, 1 = Yes	−.157 (2.35)	37.6 (3.48)		33.7 (4.34)
Head, under 24, 1 = Yes				22.1 (1.96)
Head, age 24-44, 1 = Yes	.299 (1.79)			
Head, age 45-54, 1 = Yes	.392 (2.37)		.407 (5.76)	
Head, age 55-65, 1 = Yes	.547 (3.23)		3.93 (6.11)	
Head, age 65+ 1 = Yes	.458 (2.64)		.286 (4.54)	
Current Income	.0013 (1.99)	.277 (3.21)	−.0014 (2.87)	
Calculated[b] Q_{ij}	−.0002 (.22)		.0043 (4.29)	
Moved into House, 1967-70, 1 = Yes		43.8 (3.22)		16.8 (1.70)
Calculated[b] T_{ij}		35.6 (1.70)		51.1 (2.73)
Permanent Income		.753 (6.70)	−.0021 (3.29)	.691 (9.00)
Number of Persons		.990 (.27)		
Reduced Form, R^2	.407	.387	.304	.234

[a]T_{ij} and Q_{ij} not jointly determined.
[b]Calculated from first stage of the two stage process.

jointly determined. [b] The experiments with the joint determination models were restricted to white households because of the greater sample sizes for whites. At three of the column heads the phrase "not dependent" appears, which indicates that the joint determinancy was not substantiated in the 2SLS estimates. One major problem encountered in making these estimates was the high degree of linear dependency among income, expenditures, and the subsidy variables.[c] The models shown in the table include both the subsidy and expenditure variables in those models in which they were both significant at least when included separately in the tenure function. These are the first three models; only in the model for husband-wife with head age 45-65 were both significant and of the expected sign. The subsidy variable has been omitted from the last three models as it was not significant under any of the attempted model specifications.

Thus, of the six models, there are three in which expenditures and tenure are jointly determined, but only one in which the tax subsidy in addition was jointly determined. For the other household types (husband-wife head age 30-44, and over 65 and "other families"), these results indicate the housing expenditure decision to be exogenous to that of tenure choice. In these cases the single equation model including expenditures as a determinant may be appropriate, depending on the significance of the expenditure variable.

Despite the apparent insignificance of the subsidy term in the husband-wife under age 30 model (caused by multicollinearity), we believe the effect of the subsidy to still be worthy of investigation. Also, as indicated, the subsidy measure for the 45-65 group is clearly significant.

One dramatic difference between the single equation and 2SLS estimates of the tenure probability was found for primary individuals. The 2SLS indicate housing expenditures and the tenure decision to be determined in the manner anticipated, but the relationship between income (both current and permanent) is now decidedly negative, with a mean total income elasticity of tenure choice of −0.642. Now, in the single equation estimates it was difficult to fit an income tenure relation with much confidence; the relation being found to be both positive and negative at marginal levels of significance. The 2SLS relations are highly significant and seem to be reflecting the position of many persons living alone in owner-occupied units of some value from which they cannot afford to move. One idea tested was that such persons were concentrated among the

[b]One problem encountered in estimating (A-3) when the second subsidy measure was used was the non-linearity of one of the endogenous variables. (See annex to this appendix for details.) To alleviate this problem the technique developed by H.H. Kelejian in his "Two-Stage Least Squares and Econometric Systems in Linear Parameters by Non-Linear Endogenous Variables," (*Journal of the American Statistical Association*, Vol. 66, June 1971, pp. 373-74) was used. It should also be noted that the endogenous variables included in (A-3a) were also weighted as part of the procedure to mitigate the heteroskedasticity problem.
[c]Since our interest is primarily on the determinants of tenure choice, the expenditure functions are generally not discussed.

elderly, but different relations for nonelderly versus elderly were not found in models based on "young" and "old" groups of primary individuals. All in all the negative relation between income and tenure choice indicated in the 2SLS estimates appear to be plausible, if counterintuitive. However, until a more definitive test of the negative relation can be made, it is prudent to consider the very small but positive elasticity found in the single equation model to be the norm.

Another difference in the tenure functions shown in Table A-1 from those presented in the text is the inclusion of a dummy variable indicating the household having moved into the unit since 1967 in the model for husband-wife families head age 45-65. Our first inclination was to exclude the variable from the function on the grounds that since renters as a class move more frequently than owners this variable would have the effect of explaining the probability of owner-occupants in terms of one of their dominant characteristics—lower mobility—and thus cause an identification problem. As argued in the introductory section of Chapter 4, it is likely that there are a number of characteristics which distinguish those who move from the rest of the population, only one of which is their higher propensity to rent than to own their dwelling unit. Therefore, concern over identification is mitigated in general. For this family type, unlike others in which its inclusion was tried, inclusion of the recent-move variable had very strong effects on the significance of the other variables in the function; and our conclusion is that it is controlling for variation in differences in the households other than their simply recently moving which otherwise significantly cloud the relation between tenure choice and the other independent variables.

Finally, it is of interest to note the total effect which housing expenditures have on the probability of a household being an owner-occupant. The estimates shown in Table A-2 are based on the 2SLS estimates for those three household types for which the joint determinancy of the tenure choice and expenditures was supported and on single equation models for the other three types. The table shows the total, i.e., direct and through the subsidy for those household types for which the subsidy was significant, elasticity of housing expenditure elasticity of tenure choice evaluated at the mean. (The last section of this appendix details the basis for the elasticity computation.) For younger husband-wife households and for primary individuals the elasticity is greater than unity, but for the other household types a percentage increase in expenditures only have a small effect on the probability of homeownership.

The range in these elasticities is greater than anticipated, and one reason can be advanced to explain both the range of these estimates and variance in the success of testing the joint determination model. The only tax subsidy measure which was at all significant was the ratio of housing expenditures to income. As noted at several points, the tax subsidy measure can account for factors other than subsidy. This combined with linear dependency among expenditures,

Table A-2
Housing Expenditure Elasticity of Tenure Choice

Family Type	Elasticity
Husband-Wife Head	
under age 30[a]	1.18
age 30-44[a]	3.19
age 45-65[a]	.328
Other Family	.105
Primary Individual	1.31

[a]Indicates includes direct and indirect effects of expenditures. These are household types for which the 2SLS estimates were significant.

tenure rates, income, and subsidies partially explains the high variability in the significance of these variables. It was not evident how the basic model given in (A.3) could be reformulated to avoid this basic problem. These results do, though, suggest the kinds of problems which can be anticipated in working further with joint determination models.

Alterations from Use of
Expenditures/Income to
Measure the Tax Subsidy

With federal subsidies measured as the ratio of housing expenditures to income, function (A.3) can be replaced with the identity

$$S_j = \frac{Q_{ji}}{Y_{ji}}$$

where S_j is the subsidy, Q_{ji} is expenditures, and Y_{ij} is income.
If tenure, T, is determined as

$$T = a_1 + a_2 Z + b_1 Q_{ji} + b_2 \frac{Q_{ji}}{Y_{ji}}$$

the total effect of an increment in Q_{ji} on T is

$$\frac{\partial T}{\partial Q_{ji}} = \frac{(Yb_1 + b_2)}{Y}$$

if b_1 is not significant, the effect of expenditures is b_2/Y.

Further, since it is hypothesized that the amount of housing expenditures depends, in part, on the tax subsidy, i.e.,

$$Q_{ji} = Z + Q_{ji}/Y_{ji}$$

to obtain the actual effect of some other variable, Z, on Q_{ji}, the estimated function needs to be arranged such that both Q_{ji} terms are on the left side of the equation. Then

$$\frac{\partial Q_{ji}}{\partial Z} = \frac{a_1 Y_{ij}}{(Y_{ij} - b)}$$

Appendix B:
Income Tax Advantages of
Homeownership

This appendix has two purposes which correspond to its parts. The first is to describe more comprehensively than in the text the nature of the tax advantages which accrue to those households which reside in their own homes. The second is to describe three measures of those advantages which have been specified for use in the micro models of the homeownership decision estimated in Chapter 4.

Conceptual Analysis

It is well known that considerable tax advantages accrue to homeowners, as compared to renters, from the deductibility under federal income tax statutes of certain ownership-related expenses and the failure to tax the imputed rental income from owner-occupied homes. The imputed income from an owner-occupied house is the net income which the owner could obtain by renting his residence to another household or, alternatively, by investing his equity in some other capital asset.[1] Because of his imputed income, a homeowner has less taxable income than a renter with identical earnings and assets.

Define the item which should be imputed as income, net rent (NR), to the owner occupant as

$$NR = GR - (M + D + I + T) \qquad (B.1)$$

where GR is gross rent, M is maintenance and operating expenses, D is economic obsolescence, I is mortgage interest, and T is property and other indirect taxes levied on the homeowner. If the owner-occupant were treated like other businesses (and if economic obsolescence were the depreciation concept applicable to other business) he would be required to report GR as income and be allowed to deduct $(M + D + I + T)$ as business expenses. In fact, the owner-occupant is not required to report GR but is allowed deductions in the amount $I + T$. Current tax treatment thus understates the taxable income of owner-occupants relative to other asset holders by $NR + I + T$.

It is advantageous to contrast the situation of the owner-occupant with that of the owner of rental property, whom we shall term the "landlord." The landlord's net rent, NR', is

$$NR' = GR - (M + Dep + T + I)$$

where GR is gross rental income and Dep is depreciation for tax accounting purposes. The difference between the "ideal" net rent basis for income taxation, NR, and landlord's actual tax liability, NR', is equal to $Dep - D$, or the excess of depreciation. The advantage of this difference to the landlord is t_l $(Dep - D)$, where t_l is the landlord's marginal tax rate. This contrasts with the owner-occupant's advantage of t_o $(NR + I + T)$, where t_o is the owner's marginal tax rate.[a]

In 1954 the Internal Revenue Service began allowing acceleration of depreciation up to 200 percent on rental properties owned by first owners, and up to 150 percent on properties owned by second and subsequent owners. These provisions held during the decade preceding the 1970 Census. (These provisions were altered by the Tax Reform Act of 1969.) A question of considerable import is how the acceleration in the magnitude of depreciation write-offs on rental property affected the net tax advantage of being an owner-occupant.

If the housing market is assumed to be perfectly competitive, then in the long run much of the gain from the accelerated depreciation will be passed on to renters in the form of lower rents. The fraction which is passed on depends on (a) whether the 200 percent rate or the 150 percent rate is more applicable to the majority of landlords and (b) the net benefits of the provision to the landlord, which depends on the landlords' tax brackets. Condition (a) simply indicates that there are probably windfall profits to first owners compared to other landlords;[b] condition (b) indicates those with the highest rates reap the greatest net advantage.

If renting and owning are close substitutes for some significant fraction of households, then gross rents on equivalent owner-occupied and rental properties must be quite near each other or they would be made so by households switching tenure form. Consequently, when the gross rent of rental units is reduced by a change in tax laws, then the imputed gross rent of owner-occupied units also falls. It may be, however, that the decline in the imputed rents of owner-occupied units is not as large as that of rental units since the two forms of tenure are not perfect substitutes. In terms of Equation (B.1) this means the imputed gross rent of owner-occupied units already reflects some, though not all, of the benefits which accelerated depreciation on rental properties has brought to the tenants in lower rents. For simplicity the imputed gross rent in Equation (B.1) is assumed to reflect all of the benefits of accelerated depreciation, or in other words that changes in the tax treatment of rental property affect *all* rents, actual and imputed.[c]

---

[a]To place this in perspective, contrast NR's and the deductions with the landlord's cashflow (CF) from the property which is $NR' + Dep - A$, where A is the payment to principal on the mortgage, if any.

[b]For simplicity the gains to developers from being able to deduct construction period expenses are being ignored in this analysis.

[c]This is not to say that the net advantage of owner-occupants was unaffected by accelerated depreciation provision. Since gross rents of the owner-occupied properties are lower, their net rents must also fall; in fact because property values decline, T and I will decline. For some owner-occupants NR may have become negative; but as long as $(NR + I + T) > 0$, there remains a net tax advantage to owner-occupancy. Some computations we have been able to do with admittedly crude data indicate for owner-occupants an average at least

The tax advantage of homeownership for a household from a particular dwelling clearly depends on the "gross value" of the tax advantage items associated with the dwelling and the effective tax rate faced by the households. The net value (NV) of the tax advantage to household i from property j can be expressed as

$$NV_{ij} = t_i \left[(I_j + T_j) + (\tau_{1i}^R + 0.5 \, \tau_{2i}^R) NR_j \right] \tag{B.2}$$

τ_{1i}^R and τ_{2i}^R are the fractions of investment income of a renter household in the same income class as the ith treated by the Internal Revenue Service as ordinary income and capital gains, respectively.[d] Finally, t_i is the marginal rate of the ith household.

The first component $t_i(I_j + T_j)$ accounts for the advantage from deducting mortgage interest and property tax costs of owning the home. The second component accounts for the advantage obtained through the sheltering of the current return on the investment in the house, NR_j, from tax liability.[e] Note that only the portion of NR_j which would have been paid in taxes is included in NV. The τ^R's are those of similar renter households to allow for the possible distortion of homeowners' portfolios resultant from owning the property.

To obtain a numerical estimate of Equation (B.2) two separate types of data are required: (a) data on the net rents, mortgage interest payments and other aspects of the finances of owning a home and (b) data on tax rates and investment strategies of households. Since these kinds of data are not available for the households in our Pittsburgh sample, the alternative measures, described in the next section, were specified.

Measures of the Tax Advantages of Homeowners

It is necessary to begin with a simple model of the effect which owner-occupancy has on the marginal tax rates of such occupants. Define taxable income as

NR/GR is quite low but still positive. For a description of the calculations see F. de Leeuw, D. Eisen, S.A. Marshall, and R. Struyk, "Developmental Work on The Urban Institute Housing Market Model," Washington, D.C., Urban Institute Working Paper 208-20, 1974.

[d] The tax rate on capital gains is 0.5 of the tax rate applicable on ordinary income for most households. For high income returns the tax rate is simply 25 percent of the capital gains. The qualifying income in 1969 was $52,000 for joint returns or surviving spouse, $26,000 for single returns, and $38,000 for heads of house with only one spouse present.

[e] The provisions of the tax code also favor the homeowner in the area of capital gains from his property compared to the capital gains of renters from other assets. The provision for purchasing another home within a year, the special treatment of those over sixty-five, and the provision at death all combine to make the average effective rate quite low. Whereas one can argue that such differential gains should be included on a flow basis in our accounting of tax advantages, the difficulties of making such imputations appeared to be very substantial and consequently they have not been included. This is not however, to imply that such factors are quantitatively insignificant.

gross income inclusive of imputed rental income, Y, minus deductions, D, and exemptions, E. Taxes paid (T), then are equal to the applicable tax rate (t) times and the taxable income or symbolically

$$T = t(Y - D - E) \tag{B.3}$$

Deductions can be divided between those related to homeownership and those which are not. Let the second component be represented by α, which varies among households. The deductions stemming from ownership depend primarily on the household's ratio of debt to value on the unit and on the property tax rate in the area in which the unit is located. Aggregate housing deductions are assumed to be linearly related to the value of the unit V. Hence

$$D = \alpha + BV$$

where B is the marginal rate of increase in annual deductions resulting from an increment in the value of the unit.[f] There is another housing "deduction" which has not been included in the formulation—the imputed rent from the unit. The imputed rent to the owner-occupant can be determined by multiplying the value of the unit by the net rent-value ratio, σ. Thus a more comprehensive deduction relation can be written as

$$D = \alpha + (B + \sigma)V. \tag{B.4}$$

Finally, the value of the housing unit owned and occupied by the household can be functionally related to the income of the household by

$$V = \gamma_1 + \gamma_2 Y \tag{B.5}$$

where γ_2 is the marginal propensity to buy housing stock.

By substituting (B.5) into (B.4) and the resultant (B.4) into (B.3), an expanded tax equation can be written as

$$T = tY - T\alpha - t\gamma_1(B + \sigma) - t\gamma_2(B + \sigma)Y - tE \tag{B.3$'$}$$

The change in taxes associated with an increment of income then is

$$\partial T/\partial Y = t(1 - (B + \sigma)\gamma_2). \tag{B.6}$$

---

[f]Since $V = P_k q$, where P_k is the price per unit of the housing stock and q is the number of units of housing services provided by the unit, then B can be converted to an annual equivalent by dividing it by the rate of return on the unit, i.e., $B^* = B \cdot r$. This follows from the relation determining the annual price per unit of services, i.e., $P = P_k \cdot r$.

This equation simply states that the effective tax rate confronting an owner-occupant will be reduced by the product of his "nominal" or non-ownership tax rate, the quantity composed of rate at which deductions change with the value of the unit plus the rent-value ratio, and the owner's marginal propensity to purchase housing stock.

The extent of distortion of the price of housing services is also evident from (B.6). For the renter

$$T = t(Y - \alpha - E) \text{ and } \partial T/\partial Y = t.$$

Then the price distortion is simply $t(1 - (B + \sigma)\gamma_2)$. That is, a homeowner pays at rate which is $(1 - (B + \sigma)\gamma_2)$ less than his renter counterpart.

The second subsidy measure described in the text is based directly on (B.6). Substantial evidence exists to support the contention that the income elasticity of the demand for housing services is about unity.[2] It is assumed here that income elasticity of the derived demand for housing stock is unity also. Symbolically, the assumption is

$$\gamma_2 \frac{\overline{V}}{\overline{Y}} = 1. \tag{B.7}$$

It is further assumed that the rent-value ratio (σ) and the marginal rate of increase in deductions from an increment in the value of the unit (B) do not vary across households in any systematic way.[3] These assumptions combined with (B.7), mean that γ_2 can be taken to equal the ratio of household income to home value. Thus $\partial T/\partial Y$ is directly related to the ratio of housing value or expenditures to income. This ratio is the second subsidy measure used in the analysis reported in the text. As noted in the text it has the weakness of reflecting, in addition to variations in the advantage, variations among households in their preferences for housing services versus other goods.

The first subsidy measure used in the analysis obviates the need for obtaining values or making assumptions as to values or the variability of the parameters in (B.6) by simply observing the differences in the effective tax rates paid by owner-occupants and renters with the same adjusted taxable incomes. These computations were made by Henry Aaron using the Brookings file of some 88,000 individual income tax returns.[4] One limitation of using these differences (which are reported in Table B-1) is that the published data are for relatively broad income classes.

The final tax subsidy measure was the marginal tax rate for the household based on the household's permanent income. The computation of the tax rate corresponding to the household's income is made using an estimated itemized deduction and personal exemptions. Itemized deductions for different types of

Table B-1
Difference in Federal Individual Income Tax Rates of Homeowners and Non-Homeowners Under 1966 Law

	Income Bracket (thousands of dollars)								
	Under 3	3-5	5-7	7-10	10-15	15-25	25-50	50-100	Over 100
All Returns	1.4	2.4	1.9	2.0	2.2	2.8	1.0	0.6	-0.5[a]
All Under Age 65	1.5	2.0	1.9	2.0	2.2	2.9	0.9	1.4	-0.9
Itemized Deductions	-1.8	2.1	2.7	1.7	1.8	2.5	1.6	1.4	-0.6
All Age 65 and Older	0.2	1.9	2.3	1.8	1.6	2.8	1.5	-0.4	0.1
Itemized Deductions	0.5	1.8	2.2	1.4	2.2	2.4	1.2	-0.7	0.1

[a]Minus sign indicates tax rate for homeowners is greater than that for non-homeowners.

Source: Henry Aaron, *Shelter and Subsidies* © 1972 by The Brookings Institution, Washington, D.C., p. 226, table D-4.

tax returns are published by the Internal Revenue Service.[5] These were converted into a fraction of adjusted gross income. Taxable income was determined as reported income less the estimated itemized deductions and less the value of personal exemptions. Because the income brackets for which the itemized deductions are published do not correspond with the income tax schedule brackets, the deductions could not be calculated with as much precision as might have been desired,[g] the tax rates themselves were taken from the tax schedules.

The three federal income tax schedules have been matched with the following family types given in the Census:

Federal Income Tax Schedule	Census Family Type
1. Single taxpayer	Primary individuals
2. Married couples filing jointly	All husband-wife families
3. Unmarried but household head	Other family, male or female head

The number of dependents is equal to the husband and wife (if both present) plus all those under eighteen years old living with the family plus those over sixty in a non-aged household (i.e., family head under sixty years old). Tax rates effective in 1968 were used so that the effects of the 1969 income tax reform do not enter.

---

[g]The tax schedules for single taxpayers, married taxpayers filing joint returns, and unmarried taxpayers qualifying as household heads contained 25, 25, and 32 tax brackets, respectively. After matching the brackets in the itemized deduction table with those in the schedules, 13, 12, and 12, respectively remained. The greatest loss of detail generally occurred in income brackets over $30,000, a level of income for which tax incremental considerations may not strongly effect the tenure decision.

Appendix C:
Estimation of Permanent Income

In studying the determinants of the expenditure decision of households with respect to housing or other durable goods, the desired measure of income is often the normal or permanent income of the household, i.e., income which represents the return to the household's human and non-human wealth.[1] In the present study, like most others, data on actual "permanent income" have not been available.[2] The purpose of this appendix is to describe the technique used to estimate the permanent incomes of households using the data in the 1970 Census Users' sample, which is the data used in the analysis reported in Chapter 4.[3]

The basic assumption underlying the estimates is that cross-sectional differences in family income are primarily attributable to differences in personal productivity and labor force participation of the members of the family. Thus as a first step a multiple regression analysis is performed with total family income as the dependent variable and characteristics of family members which reflect differences in productivity and labor force participation as the independent variables. The estimated regression coefficients indicate average effect which a marginal change in an attribute (e.g., an additional year of education) will have on income under normal circumstances, holding other factors constant. Substitution of the values of the independent variables for any family into the estimated regression model yields a measure of normal or permanent family income; that is, the income which the family could be expected to obtain on the basis of its marketable skills and willingness to participate in the labor force.[4]

The remainder of this appendix is taken up with the details of applying the procedure as just outlined. The first section deals with the specification of the variables in the regression model. The estimated regressions are presented and evaluated in the second section. The final section discusses the predicted permanent incomes and their relation to current incomes.

Specification of Variables

As previously noted, the dependent variable is annual family income from all sources in 1969. This includes wages and salaries, farm and non-farm business income, social security and retirement income, public assistance or welfare, and all other income. "Family" here includes primary individuals as well as husband-wife and other family types. While the attributes of the family members account for variations in income due to their productivity in the economy, all income is included as we want to estimate the permanent income of those without earnings or with income other than earnings as well as of those with strictly earned incomes. The assumption is that the level of dividend income, for example, will depend on the earner's occupation and education. The constant term in the regression will include this unearned component of income along with the effect of other phenomena, as noted below.

The estimated models include a separate set of independent variables for each "earner" in the household. "Earners" include both those who actually earned income during 1969 and certain others. In practice all husband and wives or female household heads were included as earners; other family members were included if (a) they were over eighteen years old and (b) had some income in 1969.

The following list presents the broad classes of variables included in the regression models at least on an experimental basis: (1) age, (2) age-education, (3) sex, (4) occupation, (5) veteran status, (6) number of hours and weeks worked in year, (7) work experience and constraints to working. Nearly all of these require special comment. Ages are grouped into five classes: 18-23, 24-43, 44-53, 54-64, and over 65. The age-education variables are interaction variables of the type used by Kalacheck and Raines, which they found to perform much better than the separate inclusion of education. Education is a continuous variable so that the age-education variables consist of five variables for each included family member. Veteran status and sex are additive dummy variables.

Occupation, in the sense of the type of work an employed or experienced worker performs, was included only experimentally initially, as it was possible that occupation might be explained by the age and education variables. In general, however, both sets of variables proved significant. Note that the Census provides occupation data for the employed, those in the experienced labor force, and those in the labor reserve.[a] Thus occupation data is available for anyone who had any work experience or had worked in the ten years prior to the Census. Therefore, occupation variables could be included in addition to employment status variables for nearly all groups of the population. Actual occupations have been divided into ten classes: (1) professional, technical, and managerial workers, (2) sales workers, (3) clerical and kindred workers, (4) craftsmen and kindred workers, (5) operatives except transport, (6) transport equipment operatives, (7) laborers, except farm, (8) farmers and farm laborers, (9) service workers except private household, and (10) private household workers. For a given "earner," the dummy variable for this occupation takes the value of one, and the other nine are zero.

The final set of variables attempts to pursue the labor force participation aspect of the estimation of permanent income somewhat further than the indication of labor force status at the time of the Census as this point-in-time indication may be misleading. Some indications of work history and constraints

---

[a]Exact definitions of selected variables appear in Table C-6; and the final section of this appendix.

are sought, the assumption being that those who have worked in the past and/or who are currently constrained from working by familial responsibility may have a higher earnings capacity as a result of their experience. To account for the work history, for those over twenty-three a dummy variable is included indicating whether they were employed five years ago or not, either full or part time. Those attending college or in the military are treated as being employed, for simplicity. This work experience variable is in addition to that implicitly included in the occupational variables which detect long or permanent absence from the labor force while the five-year tests picks up more recent experience. The Census also includes the year in which those listed as unemployed or not in the labor force last worked for pay. This information has been included as a three-level dummy variable, relative to having never worked: 1970-1967, 1960-67, and 1959 or earlier. Finally, the presence of children under age six is included to account for the increased opportunity cost of working outside of the home. This variable enters for the entire household, not for individual members.

Of interest equal to the historical labor force participation of workers is the intensity of their current work effort. To capture this the number of weeks worked in the previous year has been included as a two-level dummy variable, with the base being full time (over 47 weeks) employment; the classes are under 26 weeks and 27-47 weeks. Part-time work on a consistent basis is accounted for by a dummy variable for those who work less than thirty-five hours a week.

Race has not been included as an independent variable because it is believed that race enters into the determination of income in a complicated manner, not only with respect to earned income but income from wealth or transfer payments. For this reason separate regression models were estimated for blacks and whites.

Some idea of the characteristics of the sample households which are relevant for the estimation of permanent income is available from the mean values of selected variables given in Table C-1. There are sharp differences between the "earners" of the same race and between the earners of different races.

Estimated Regression Models

The "final form" of the regression model explaining total family income for white Pittsburgh households in 1970 is presented in Table C-2. The table presents the results for a single model and the four columns present the coefficients of household variables and variables for each of the three earners, respectively. All coefficients have the expected sign and are of the proper order of magnitude. The model "explains" about 35 percent of the variance in total family incomes, which is consistent with other similar studies.

The constant term contains two separate components. One part is the mean unearned income. The second part is the value of earned income when all of the

Table C-1

Mean Values of Selected Variables for Included Households and Earners

	White Households			Black Households		
A. Household Characteristics						
Total family income	11564			6460		
No. of "earners"[a]	1.844			1.654		
Children under age 6	.298			.325		
B. Earner[a] Characteristics						
	Earner			Earner		
	1	2	3	1	2	3
Fraction female	.146	.929	.393	.277	1.0	.513
Age distribution						
under 24	.053	.081	.733	.081	.103	.873
24-44	.336	.393	.125	.343	.382	–
45-54	.252	.245	.011	.250	.257	–
55-65	.240	.168	.044	.184	.180	–
over 65	.119	.113	.087	.142	.078	.127
Years of school	13.71	12.75	14.26	11.83	12.45	13.94
Occupation distribution[b]						
Professional, manager	.277	.098	.062	.063	.060	–
Sales	.074	.060	.125	.024	.060	.062
Clerical	.123	.210	.180	.142	.146	.187
Craftsmen	.216	.005	.087	.096	.005	–
Operatives, expt. transpt.	.112	.039	.106	.172	.085	.124
Transpt operatives	.051	.001	.030	.054	–	.062
Laborers	.044	.005	.169	.169	.015	.124
Farmer or farm worker	.001	.001	–	.003	–	–
Service worker	.100	.091	.224	.209	.185	.336
Domestic	.003	.004	.011	.098	.075	.062
Fraction unemployed or not in labor force[b]	.152	.259	.934	.283	.282	1.0
Distribution of weeks worked for those working in 1969[b]						
under 26	.052	.097	.594	.099	.150	.876
26-47	.090	.084	.161	.169	.095	.062
Fraction of unemployed working under 35 hours per week[b]	.086	.095	–	.090	.094	–
Number of earners	3030	2538	143	332	199	16

[a]See text for definition of those included as "earners."

[b]See the final section of Appendix C for exact definitions.

Table C-2

Estimation of Total Family Income for White Pittsburgh Households in 1970—Final Form

	Household		Earner 1		Earner 2		Earner 3	
Dependent Variable: Total Family Income in Hundreds of Dollars								
	Coeff.	t-stat.	Coeff.	t-stat.	Coeff.	t-stat.	Coeff.	t-stat.
Constant	83.4	6.41						
No. of children <6	−6.17	2.23						
Under age 24								
age dummy			−20.8	.55	−13.6	.34		
age-education			−.71	.29	.64	.24		
Age 24-44								
age dummy			−30.4	2.27	−22.8	1.27		
age-education			1.56	1.88	3.41	2.91		
Age 45-54								
age dummy			−120.00	14.3	−48.7	2.62		
age-education			9.40	.95	5.47	4.25		
Age 55-65								
age dummy			−57.7	11.3	−46.0	3.17		
age-education			5.14	.8	5.71	5.49		
Female, 1 = yes			−28.8	5.62	6.08	.84		
Unemp. or not in labor force, 1 = yes			−31.3	6.18	−13.7	4.03		
Weeks worked Under 26, 1 = yes			−30.0	5.13	−8.15	1.78		
26-47, 1 = yes			−15.4	3.63				
Unemp. last worked 67-70, 1 = yes			13.9	2.65			19.2	2.65
Veteran, 1 = yes					58.6	2.45		
Occupation								
professional			45.5	12.1	17.0	3.46		
sales			18.9	3.78			28.6	1.84
craftsmen			7.85	2.25			44.0	2.43
clerk			8.78	2.06				
operative							24.6	1.47
transport. opert.			9.87	1.72				

$\bar{R}^2$	.352
SEE	64.4
F	46.84
n	3035

independent variables are zero. In the model in Table C-2 this is the value of the base dummy variables; for example, for the first earner this is a male over age sixty-five, working full time in an occupation not explicitly included for this "earner." It is not possible to disentangle these two components from the estimates we have made.[b]

Some care should be exercised in using the effect on family income of a worker of a given age having attended school for a particular number of years. As noted, the omitted age category is over age sixty-five. Most "earners" over sixty-five are retired. However, the effect on earnings of not being in the labor force has been explicitly controlled for in the model, so that to get the effect of the included age-education variables relative to a retired earner one needs to take account of the appropriate (i.e., for the corresponding "earner") "not being in the labor force" variable. A further complication is the interdependence between education and occupation variables which strongly effect the coefficients 'of both sets of variables. Below are listed the family income increments (in thousands of dollars) associated with several age-education categories based on a model excluding occupation variables and adjusted so as to make the comparison with retired age "earners":[c]

| | Earner 1 | | Earner 2 | |
| | Years of School | | Years of School | |
Age	12	16	12	16
24-44	1.32	3.00	2.85	5.04
45-54	−.260	6.70	2.64	5.73
55-65	3.25	6.32	3.33	6.25

The age and age-education variables for those under twenty-four were not significant. For the sixteen years of school case, the age-education curve has the normally expected shape. For the twelve years of school case, the early (age 24-44) peak in earnings combined with the late (age 54-65) peak give a U-shaped relation that is consistent with findings of Rees and Schultz for semi-skilled workers when seniority was considered.[5] With the heavily unionized labor force in Pittsburgh, the U shape for those with moderate schooling is expected.

The final form of the regression model determining family income of black Pittsburgh households in 1970 is presented in Table C-3. The model explains

[b]Decomposition would require one to estimate a model identical to that in Table C-2 for earned income only to determine the value of the second component of the constant described in the text. Then if one assumed that the independent variables were uncorrelated with unearned income, the mean value of unearned income could be determined by subtracting the constant in Table C-2 from that from the estimated model for earned income only.

[c]Variables for earners 1 and 2 besides age, age-education, and unemployment included in the model were: female, worked under 26 weeks, worked 26-47 weeks (earner 1 only), worked in 68-70 (earners 1 and 3), veteran (earner 2 only), and the number of children in the household.

about 37 percent of the variance in total family income. The age-education variables did not perform well in this model; inclusion of age and education variables
for the second earners, who were in all cases female, did not have a significant
impact on family income.[d] The age variables for the first earner imply maximum
income at age fifty-three, with the overall relation having an inverted U shape.
No variables for the third earners were significant, probably because all of them
were unemployed or not in the labor force at the time of the Census and 87
percent had worked fewer than twenty-six weeks in the previous year.[e]

Computation of Permanent Income

Given the estimated regression models just reviewed, the actual calculation of
permanent income is fairly direct. The basic procedure is to obtain a "calculated" income for each household using its values of the independent variables.

In two respects, however, we have departed from this basic procedure. First,
we have assigned all households to the same age category to abstract from the
life-cycle earnings pattern. This amounts to summarizing lifetime expected income in a single measure.[f] This is the simplest of a number of assumptions which
might have been made, but for the analysis of Chapter 4 this measure seemed
generally sufficient.[g]

[d]For models including only age and education variables, this was not the case, but in more
complete models they were consistently insignificant.

[e]The constant term in this model is not significantly different from zero which is somewhat
surprising as a positive value is expected a priori. Expanding on the earlier discussion, the
constant can be thought of as consisting of three components: b_1 is the "pure" constant,
the value of the constant in the absence of any dummy variables—it might be thought of as
the earnings of the earner with the lowest quantity of human capital; b_2 is the value of
earnings of the base "earner" as defined by the dummy variables; b_3 is mean unearned
income. Now our assumption is that $b_3 \geqslant 0$ and $b_2 > 0$. For this result to be consistent with
the regression result requires that the "earner" with the minimum capital have negative
earnings. Put differently it says that only workers with greater than minimum capital can
obtain employment in even the lowest paying jobs. For the estimated constant to equal zero
requires $-b_1 = b_2 + b_3$.

[f]The major objection to using this procedure to compute the lifetime expected income of
the household is the change in the number of earners which likely occurs over the life time.
To take a simple example, a husband-wife family in later years could easily lose one of its
members. Our computation of permanent income of the single-individual household would
be based only on the one individual's earning characteristics, which is clearly inappropriate.
The problems, though, of attempting to follow the demographic history of "typical"
families and applying these to individual cases are very great. So as a constrained solution,
use of this measure of expected life-time income seemed justified.

[g]It would be a simple matter, though, to modify the procedure outlined below to
correspond to different planning or decision periods. One might, for example, wish to
determine the expected income of a household over the ten-year period beginning in the
year in which the household purchased a major durable good.
To obtain such estimates one would calculate expected incomes for each year or age
group as required using the estimated regression model. In these calculations only the
variables for the age of the earners and the labor force participation and unemployment
rates associated with that race, sex, and age would change. The expected income over the
period, then, is the average of calculated incomes. The average could also be weighted or
discounted as thought appropriate.

Table C-3

Estimation of Total Family Income for Black Pittsburgh Households in 1970—Final Form

Dependent Variable: Total Family Income in Hundreds of Dollars		
	Coefficient	t-statistic
Constant	1.70	.08
"Earner 1"		
Age	2.11	2.65
Age squared	−.020	2.33
Years of school	1.52	2.08
Female	−29.5	6.15
Unemployed or not in labor force	−20.0	4.00
Worked under 26 weeks	−16.6	2.40
Occupation		
professional	10.5	1.21
clerical worker	11.5	1.97
craftsmen	9.0	1.33
"Earner 2"		
Unemployed or not in labor force	−13.8	2.33
Occupation		
professional	28.1	2.57
clerical worker	33.6	4.62
operative	24.1	2.56
service worker	22.3	3.24
$\bar{R}^2$	.371	
SEE	34.1	
F	15.1	
n	332	

In the present calculations all households have been assigned to same age category. All white workers were assigned to the 45-54 year old group, and all blacks were treated as being age 50. The choice of age was arbitrary; the one chosen should generally give peak life time earnings. Age assignments are made only for those earners whose age significantly affected family income.

A second adjustment to the procedure of simply substituting the values of the independent variables for a household into the model concerns the treatment of unemployment, absence from the labor force, and part-time work. As indicated earlier, we have estimated a joint income-labor force participation model. It is evident that unemployment, non-participation in the labor force, and working part time are all statuses which different individuals occupy at varying points in their lives and for varying lengths of time. It is inappropriate, thus, when estimating permanent income to simply assign to any worker the status he occupies at the time of the Census. To account for the temporal variations in employment status we have assumed that among sex-race groups of the population, the probability of having a given employment status is the average probability for that group. As an example, the average probability of a white male being unemployed or not in the labor force in 1970 in Pittsburgh was 0.179; it is this probability value which is used for this independent variable for all white males (multiplied by the appropriate coefficient) in computing permanent total family income. Table C-4 shows the groups and the average probabilities used. Note that the probabilities of working less than full time are independent of employment status (i.e., the first entry and the sum of the second and third entries in each column below should be less than unity). Greater precision as to the age groups within each of the groups shown would have been desirable; unfortunately, the detailed economic and social characteristics from the 1970 Census for Pennsylvania were not available at the time of these computations.

To summarize, in calculating permanent income, all workers were assigned the same age or age class and all were assigned the average probability of being out of work or working part time in their sex-race group. All other characteristics of the household and "earners" are unchanged. Thus, for example, in the age-education interaction variables in the model for white households, the age bracket is the same for all earners, but the years of school are that of the individual earner.

The results of estimating permanent income are summarized in Table C-5, which gives the means and coefficients of variation of current and permanent income by race and household type. As expected, the coefficients of variation are smaller for permanent income than for current income for all household types. Differences in mean income by family type reflect differences in

Table C-4
Employment Status by Race and Sex

| | Group and Probability | | | |
| | Whites | | Blacks | |
Employment Status	Male	Female	Male	Female
Unemployed or Not in Labor Force	.179	.598	.302	.563
Employed Working under 26 Weeks	.118	.278	.161	.283
Employed Working 26-47 Weeks	.185	.261	.241	.261

Source: U.S. Bureau of the Census, *1970 Census Economic and Social Characteristics of the Population*, Tables 81, 82, 83.

Table C-5

Summary Statistics of Current and Permanent Income by Household Type for Pittsburgh Households, 1970

A. White Households

Family Type	Current Income (hundreds of dollars)			Permanent Income (hundreds of dollars)		
	Mean	Std. Dev.	Coeff. Var.	Mean	Std. Dev.	Coeff. Var.
Husband-Wife,						
Head under age 30	102.5	54.6	53.2	140.4	53.0	37.7
Head, 30-44	124.5	68.0	54.6	129.0	48.4	37.5
Head, 45-65	143.5	86.8	60.5	112.7	51.0	45.2
Head over 65	101.1	97.6	96.5	94.7	56.2	59.2
Other Family	91.0	58.5	64.3	123.7	80.0	64.5
Primary Individuals	61.0	59.0	96.7	68.4	48.9	71.5
All Households	115.6	80.1	69.3	106.2	58.5	55.1

B. Black Households

	Current Income (hundreds of dollars)			Permanent Income (hundreds of dollars)		
	Mean	Std. Dev.	Coeff. Var.	Mean	Std. Dev.	Coeff. Var.
Husband-Wife, head under age 45	82.2	37.3	45.4	74.4	16.8	22.6
Husband-Wife, head over 44	80.0	43.2	54.0	67.2	16.2	24.1
Other Family	49.4	42.8	86.6	41.4	16.1	38.9
Primary Individual	35.6	31.0	87.1	47.6	19.5	41.0
All Households	64.6	44.0	68.1	59.2	21.6	36.5

educational attainment, occupational distribution, and race but *not* differences in age or employment status. The reduction in variance between current and permanent income is especially striking for black households. The lower variances reflect the little effect which the age and education of "second earners" and many occupations for both "earners" have on the total family income of blacks. Finally, the detail on family type in the table shows that the greater variance observed in the current incomes of non-husband-wife households is carried over into the estimates of permanent incomes.

In terms of the crude checks on the overall sensibility of the permanent income estimates, the data in Table C-5 indicate the method outlined to be capable of providing "reasonable" estimates. Unfortunately, there are no independent data on permanent income for these households with which to confront our estimates.[6]

Definitions of Selected Variables[7]

1. Years of School: Highest grade ever attended; does not imply completion of this grade.
2. Hours Worked per Week: Respondents who indicated working during the reference week were asked how many hours they worked this week at all jobs excluding time off and including overtime or extra hours.
3. Year Last Worked: Coded for respondents *not* indicating being (a) at work, (b) in the Armed Forces, (c) with a job but not at work. Respondents were asked when they last worked at all, even for a few days, including unpaid work on family farm or in family business.
4. Weeks Worked: Determined for those who worked at all during the calendar year preceding the Census. Question asked how many weeks were worked either part time or full time; paid vacations, paid sick leave, and military service are counted as weeks worked.
5. Unemployed or Not in Labor Force: (1) Unemployed—those civilians age 14 and over who were neither at work nor with a job but not at work during the reference week, who were also looking for work within the past 60 days. (2) Not in labor force—includes all those not (a) employed, (b) unemployed, and (c) in the Armed Forces plus those persons doing incidental (less than 15 hours per week) unpaid work on a family farm or business.
6. Occupation: Determined for persons 14 years of age and over in the experienced civilian labor force or in the labor reserve. Employed persons reported the occupation at which they worked the most hours during the reference week. The experienced unemployed (unemployed persons who have worked at some time in the past) and persons in the labor reserve (those not in the labor force but who had worked within the past 10 years) reported their last occupation. This, therefore, excludes jobless persons who last worked over 10 years ago.
7. Veterans: Civilian *males* (not on active military duty) who have served in the U.S. Armed Forces, regardless of whether their service was in wartime or peacetime.

More precise definitions of the ten occupation categories are given in Table C-6.

Table C-6
Definitions of the Ten Occupation Categories

	Description	Census Code Numbers
1.	Professional, technical and kindred workers, plus managers and administrative except farm	001-246
2.	Sales workers	260-296
3.	Clerical and kindred workers	301-396
4.	Craftsmen and kindred workers	401-596
5.	Operatives, except transport	601-696
6.	Transport equipment operatives	701-726
7.	Laborers, except farm	740-796
8.	Farmers, farm managers, farm foremen, and farm laborers	801-846
9.	Service workers, except private households	901-976
10.	Private household workers	980-986

Appendix D:
Regression Estimates of
Cross-SMSA Income-Tenure
Choice Model

Table D-1
Regression Estimates of Basic Model for Black and White Households by Household Type[a]

	Husband-Wife Families, Head				Other Family	Primary Individ.	All Households
	Under Age 30	Age 30-44	Age 45-65	Over Age 65			
	A. Black Households						
α	6.063	6.783	6.875	6.938	6.597	6.447	6.619
t-ratio	(26.0)	(94.6)	(112)	(66.6)	(45.0)	(29.8)	(65.6)
β	−.312	−.214	−.154	−.092	−.151	−.112	−.127
t-ratio	(3.63)	(6.08)	(5.95)	(4.82)	(6.32)	(4.65)	(6.10)
R^2	.328	.578	.567	.462	.597	.445	.579
$\bar{R}^2$	.303	.563	.551	.442	.582	.425	.564
F	13.2	37.0	35.4	23.2	39.9	21.7	37.2
n	29	29	29	29	29	29	29
	B. White Households						
α	6.303	6.930	6.869	6.723	6.596	5.915	6.805
t-ratio	(81.5)	(217.)	(732.)	(500.)	(103.)	(83.6)	(164.)
β	−.369	−.272	−.127	−.053	−.236	−.031	−.192
t-ratio	(9.26)	(9.13)	(16.9)	(8.42)	(6.33)	(2.99)	(9.19)
R^2	.722	.716	.899	.780	.556	.473	.707
$\bar{R}^2$	.714	.708	.896	.769	.542	.420	.699
F	85.7	83.3	284.	71.0	40.0	8.96	84.5
n	35	35	34	22	34	12	37

[a]Dependent variable is the (arithmetic mean of the fraction of households who are owner occupants in an SMSA $*1000$).

Table D-2
Basic Tenure Income Relationship, Both Races Combined

Husband-Wife Family Types, Head

	Under Age 30		Age 30-44		Age 44-65		Over Age 65	
	$lnGM^a$	$lnAM^b$	$lnGM^a$	$lnAM^b$	$lnGM^a$	$lnAM^b$	$lnGM^a$	$lnAM^b$
α	6.267	6.291	6.891	6.924	6.840	6.858	6.711	6.754
t-ratio	(79.1)	(85.0)	(105)	(225)	(275)	(717)	(529)	(468)
β	−.386	−.375	−.475	−.285	−.214	−.127	−.055	−.036
t-ratio	(9.15)	(9.99)	(8.01)	(10.3)	(11.1)	(17.2)	(9.44)	(5.36)
R^2	.705	.740	.647	.752	.791	.900	.817	.590
$\bar{R}^2$	.697	.733	.637	.745	.784	.897	.807	.570
F	83.7	99.8	64.1	106.	124.	29.7	89.1	28.8
n	37	37	37	37	36	36	22	22

	Primary Individuals		Other Families		All Households Combined	
	$lnGM^a$	$lnAM^b$	$lnGM^a$	$lnAM^b$	$lnGM^a$	$lnAM^b$
α	5.8942	5.9254	6.598	6.5135	6.776	6.766
t-ratio	(95.9)	(58.6)	(124)	(116)	(95)	(152)
β	−.028	−.036	−.221	−.231	−.227	−.176
t-ratio	(3.09)	(2.40)	(7.49)	(7.40)	(6.86)	(8.51)
R^2	.489	.367	.623	.617	.573	.674
$\bar{R}^2$	.438	.303	.612	.606	.561	.665
F	9.58	5.79	56.1	54.8	47.0	72.5
n	12	12	36	36	37	37

[a] Natural log of (geomatric mean of fraction of households owner-occupants) *1000.
[b] Natural log of (arithmetic mean of fraction of households owner-occupants) *1000.

Appendix E:
Notes of the Determinants
of X_j

The low degree of variance in X_j explained by the reduced-form models presented in the body of this volume was contrary to our expectations. Examination of the residuals of the estimated models suggested that part of the unexplained variance might be associated with differences in the cost of land across metropolitan areas. In general one would expect areas with high land costs to use each parcel more intensively, and in the reduced form estimates this effect should be partially reflected in the coefficient of the percent of units in single unit structures variable. Since Muth has estimated the elasticity of substitution of non-land factors for land in the production of housing to be less than unity,[1] it is possible for land costs to exert an influence separate from that of structure type. Higher land costs will be sharply reflected in higher capital costs of owner-occupied housing; these, in turn, have a particularly strong effect on homeownership because they increase the initial capital required for home purchase, i.e., the downpayment.

To test the effect of the variation in land prices on X_j two additional variables were included in the regressions explaining X_j. The first is the ratio of capital costs to operating costs of owner-occupied housing (P_c/P_o) taken from the BLS intermediate family budget. (Data on the price of housing services relative to other goods (P_h/P_t) are from the same source.) The second variable is the price per square foot of land of existing homes (P_1) as calculated by the FHA for homes which it has insured under its Section 203 program in 1969.[2]

The estimated regression models are given in Table E-1. Two basic forms of the model are included. In the first (regressions (1), (2), and (5)) the variables describing the housing stock and market size are replaced with the relative price of housing services (P_h/P_t). In the second form, which is similar to those presented in the text, the market size and stock characteristics variables are included. In this specification the family type variables and variables measuring residential segregation have been excluded as they were, at best, only marginally significant. Both specifications include mean household income.

The regressions in the first four columns of the table are of interest at this point. Under the first form (col. 2) only P_1 has a marginally significant effect on X_j due to the substantial linear dependency between P_c/P_o and P_1 ($r = 0.6$).[a] Both P_c/P_o and P_1 have the expected effect of increasing X_j. In the second specification, in which only P_1 is included along with the stock characteristics variables (col. 4), there is a substantial increase in the portion of the variance of X_j which is accounted for over that in the basic model (col. 3). Thus, higher land prices do significantly raise the level of income required for a given rate of

[a] Both (P_c/P_o) and P_1 were highly significant when included separately in this model.

Table E-1
Further Regression Results for X_j, All Households Combined

	Dependent Variable X_j						
	(1)	(2)	(3)	(4)	(5)	(6)	(7)
Constant	-21243 (2.32)	-17142 (1.83)	10028 (.96)	7743 (.79)	234.6 (.02)	14284 (1.55)	12012 (1.44)
Mean household income	1.85 (2.90)	1.72 (2.74)	1.46 (2.31)	1.25 (2.08)	1.58 (2.82)	1.58 (2.85)	1.37 (2.71)
P_h/P_t	8526 (1.47)	6102 (1.04)		1072	1072 (.20)		
P_c/P_o	2929 (1.70)	1414 (.72)			1090 (.63)		
P_1		2943 (1.55)		3603 (2.25)	2839 (1.68)		3881 (2.88)
Percent units in 1-unit structures			-144.8 (2.36)	-111.8 (1.88)		-71.2 (1.22)	-32.4 (.60)
Percent units built before 1940			-116.3 (2.76)	-99.1 (2.45)		-94.1 (2.50)	-74.6 (2.16)
Number of units in housing market			-.0002 (.21)	-.0008 (.80)		-.0008 (.85)	-.0013 (1.66)
Percent units owner-occupied in 1940					-255.2 (3.09)	-279.2 (3.23)	-291.7 (3.74)
$\bar{R}^2$	.341	.368	.388	.456	.501	.527	.617
F	7.21	6.24	6.70	7.04	8.23	9.01	10.6

owner-occupancy in an urban area. Presumably this results from the greater savings requirement it imposes on owner-occupants, although it may reflect other factors as well. The more fundamental question, though, is what accounts for the variation in land prices among areas. Until there is better evidence on this issue, drawing strong implications for its effects on tenure choice may be questionable.

Another hypothesis as to the still comparatively low degree of variance in X_j which we have been able to explain is that the variance in X_j across cities which we presently observe results in part from the variance in the "tradition" of homeownership among cities. We will define "traditional" ownership rates as those which existed prior to the Second World War, and 1940 ownership rates are used for this purpose. Recall that before the war the effects of the creation of the Federal Housing Administration and FNMA had had little effect in reducing the high down payment and short mortgage periods which were common practice until the late 1940s. Thus prior to 1940 differences in owner-occupancy may have been much more closely associated with the customs of particular nationalities—both in the taste for owner occupancy and in savings habits—than after the war when homeownership became easier and more common.

Assuming that such factors significantly influenced homeownership in the prewar period, the way in which they effect the current ease of ownership remains to be addressed. Three effects seem fairly direct. First, the early demand for homeownership would have fostered the growth of local financial institutions with special interest in investing in mortgages. Despite the eventual formation of a national secondary market in mortgage paper, the existence of such local institutions may still be an important factor, especially for certain higher risk conventional mortgages and for ethnic-oriented banks. Second, nationalities displaying a high preference for ownership and/or a high degree of thrift will likely develop a reputation for "dependability" and "reliability" in the community. Again, this may have the effect of extending a line of credit to some households which do not meet the normal industry "rules of thumb." Finally, there is little question that an early, high incidence of homeownership resulted in a greater fraction of dwelling units being in single-unit structures which provided a stock of such units to satisfy later demand for owner-occupancy in such units, although this aspect should already be accounted for by the structure variable included in the model.

To test the importance of the "ownership heritage" the percentage of occupied units which were owner-occupied in each area in 1940 was calculated using the 1970 definitions of the included metropolitan areas. The results of adding this variable to the two basic regression models are shown in columns (5)-(7) of Table E-1. For both specifications the effect is to significantly increase the portion of the variance of X_j explained by the models; the final model explains over 60 percent of the variance in X_j

adjusted for degrees of freedom. As anticipated, though, the significance of the variable for the fraction of units in single unit structures is greatly reduced by adding the 1940 ownership rate.[b]

Overall, the "ownership heritage" hypothesis seems to be supported. It is clear, however, that the interpretation given above to the significance of the 1940 ownership rate is not the only one which might be advanced. One might argue, for example, that a certain continuity in ownership patterns is all that has been established, and therefore the causal interpretation is unwarranted. Although this argument is rejected because the enormous change in the number and composition of households in the postwar period could have produced radical changes in tenure in urban areas, the uncertainty of our explanation remains. For this reason we have chosen to include these results only provisionally in this appendix.

---

[b]The simple correlation of the percentage of units in single unit structures, with the fraction of units owner occupied in 1940, is 0.43, significant at the 5 percent level. The correlation between the percent units in single unit structures and land costs was −0.28, insignificant at the 5 percent level.

Appendix F:
An Aggregate Model of Tenure Choice, Housing Consumption, and Housing Supply in a Metropolitan Area

The variable definitions developed in Chapter 3 are employed here with the following exceptions:

Q_o is the aggregate probability of owner tenure

Q_r is the aggregate probability of rental tenure ($= 1 - Q_o$)

Q_o^q is the average housing services purchased by owner-occupant households

Q_r^q is the average housing services purchased by rental households

Q is the aggregate housing services purchased in the market

H_o is the number of owner-occupant households

H_r is the number of renter households

Q_d^k is the average housing stock demanded by homeowners.

Additionally, let Y, fam, and W be the distributions of these factors across all households instead of the values for individual households; R_y, γ and β_y have the average values for all owner-occupant households. The subscripts o or r on some variables mean that these refer only to the subpopulation who are owner-occupants or renter households.

$$Q_o = a_1 + a_2 lnP + a_3 \text{fam} + a_4 \text{race} + a_5 [SP_{so} - P_{sr}] \qquad (F.1)$$
$$+ a_6 (P_{so} - \Pi) + a_7 Q_d^k$$

$$Q/H = b_1 + b_2 Y + b_3 \text{fam} + b_4 \text{race} + b_5 (P - \Pi) + b_6 H \qquad (F.2)$$

$$Q_o^q = c_1 + c_2 Y_o + c_3 \text{fam}_o + c_4 \text{race}_o + c_5 (SP_{so} - P_{sr}) \qquad (F.3)$$
$$+ c_6 (P_{so} - \Pi) + c_7 Q_d^k$$

$$P_k = d_1 + d_2 P_c + d_3 Q + d_4 Q_d^k \qquad (F.4)$$

$$Q_d^k = e_1 + e_2 Q_o^q + e_3 r_o + e_4 r + e_5 W_o \qquad (F.5)$$

177

$$P_{so} = f_1 + f_2 P_k + f_3 Q_o^q + f_4 P_o + f_5 M + f_6 Q + f_7 E \tag{F.6}$$

$$P_{sr} = g_1 + g_2 P_c + g_3 P_o + g_4 Q_r^q + g_5 M + g_6 Q + g_7 E \tag{F.7}$$

$$r_o \equiv \frac{P_{so} - P_o}{P_k} - d \tag{F.8}$$

$$S \equiv \beta_Y (\gamma (P_{so} Q_o^q) + R_y)/Q_o^q P_{so} \tag{F.9}$$

$$Q_r \equiv 1 - Q_o \tag{F.10}$$

$$H_o \equiv Q_o H \tag{F.11}$$

$$H_r \equiv H - H_o \tag{F.12}$$

$$P \equiv (P_{so} \cdot H_o + P_{sr} \cdot H_r)/H \tag{F.13}$$

$$Q_r^q = (Q - H_o Q_o^q)/H_r \tag{F.14}$$

The total number of households in the market, H, which in one dimension defines the size of the market, is exogenous to the system as to make it endogenous would involve incorporating central-place or differential regional growth theory in the model. H_o and H_r, the fraction of households owning and renting, are determined within the system through equations F.1, F.11 and F.12. The implicit assumption in these identities is that there is a single household for each dwelling unit, a quite reasonable assumption in the urban United States.

Notes

Notes

Notes to Chapter 1
Introduction

1. The most recent contribution to this literature, which contains a partial bibliography to earlier efforts, is Geoffrey Carliner, "Income Elasticity of Housing Demand," *Review of Economics and Statistics* 55 (November 1973): 528-32. For references to empirical work on the supply elasticity of housing services see the first section of Chapter 3.

2. For a review of the essential properties of these models see Mahlon R. Straszheim, *An Econometric Analysis of the Urban Housing Market* (New York: National Bureau of Economic Research, 1975), Chapter 2; and Edwin Mills, *Studies in the Structure of the Urban Economy* (Baltimore: Johns Hopkins Press, 1972), Chapter 4.

3. See Victoria Lapham, "Race and Housing: A Review of the Issues," in G.M. von Furstenberg, B. Harrison, and A.R. Horowitz (eds.), *Patterns of Racial Discrimination*, Vol. I, *Housing* (Lexington, Massachusetts: Lexington Books, D.C. Heath and Company, 1974).

4. One very recent exception to this is C.D. MacRae and R. Struyk, "FHA, Tenure Choice, and Residential Land Use," Washington, D.C., Urban Institute Working Paper 216-3, 1975.

Notes to Chapter 2
Basic Numbers on Urban Homeownership

1. For additional discussion of aggregate homeownership based on national data see Geoffrey Carliner, "Determinants of Home Ownership," Madison, Wisconsin, University of Wisconsin, Institute for Research on Poverty Discussion Paper 169-73, June 1973.

2. For more on the variation in rent-value ratios, see R. Struyk and S.A. Marshall, "Regional Variations in Housing Attribute Prices," *Northwest Regional Science Review* 4 (1974): 51-59.

Notes to Chapter 3
A General Framework

1. The concept of housing as a homogeneous good was first stated by R.F. Muth in "The Demand for Non-Farm Housing," in A. Harbengen (ed.), *The Demand for Durable Goods* (Chicago: Chicago University Press, 1960), pp.

29-96. An amplification of the basic concept is given by E.O. Olsen, "A Competitive Theory of the Housing Market," *American Economic Review*, 1969, pp. 612-22.

2. For a review of the form and results of estimating the consumption demand for housing services see Frank de Leeuw, "The Demand for Housing: A Review of the Cross-Section Evidence," *Review of Economics and Statistics*, February 1971, pp. 1-10. Also see the comment on this article by S. Maisel, J. Burnham, and J.S. Austin, "The Demand for Housing: A Comment," *Review of Economics and Statistics*, November 1971.

3. These points are amplified and tested in John Bossons, "Credit Rationing, Indivisibilities, Portfolio Balance Effects, and the Wealth Elasticity of the Demand for Housing," Toronto, University of Toronto, unpublished paper, 1973.

4. The concavity will also increase as the level of income rises. For a discussion and estimates of the magnitude of the federal tax advantages of homeownership see Henry Aaron, "Income Taxes and Housing," *American Economic Review*, December 1970, pp. 789-806. The components of the tax advantages to homeowners are examined in Appendix B of this paper.

5. For a critical evaluation of the advantages of homeownership for renters at the lower end of the income distribution, see Peter Marcuse, "Homeownership for the Poor: Economic Implications for the Owner/Occupant," Washington, D.C., Urban Institute Working Paper No. 112-26, 1971.

6. A Theoretical argument in favor of this hypothesis is given in James L. Sweeney, "Housing Unit Maintenance and the Mode of Tenure," *Journal of Economic Theory* 8 (1974): 111-38.

7. For a further discussion of this point see R. Struyk and L. Ozanne, "Conceptual Analysis of Landlords and Owner-Occupants as Suppliers of Housing Services," Washington, D.C., Urban Institute Working Paper 221-02, 1975.

8. F. de Leeuw assisted by N. Ekanem "Time Lags in the Rental Housing Market," *Urban Studies*, 1973, pp. 39-68.

9. For an extended discussion of the income, family, and life cycle determinants see Daniel Fredland, "Residential Mobility and Choice of Tenure," in John F. Kain (ed.), *The NBER Simulation Model, Vol. II: Supporting Empirical Studies* (New York: National Bureau of Economic Research, 1970) (mimeo), p. 112.

10. Although Wyatt Mankin argues that the relatively high costs of ownership in multi-family dwellings make ownership of single-unit structures less desirable on economic grounds as well as for reasons of taste, in his empirical tests structural characteristics are omitted. See his *Ownership and Race*, Urban Economics Report No. 35 (Chicago: University of Chicago, 1971), processed. One recent exception to this is the work by Kain and Quigley cited in note 11.

11. For a discussion of some of the financial factors limiting black ownership

of housing, see John F. Kain, *Theories of Residential Location and Realities of Race*, Harvard-MIT Program of Regional and Urban Economics, Discussion Paper No. 47, Cambridge, June 1960; a more general discussion of factors affecting the supply elasticity of housing to the segregated poor, see Martin Bailey, "Note on the Economics of Residential Zoning and Urban Renewal," *Land Economics*, August 1959, pp. 288-92. For evidence on the importance of the structure type available in segregated areas for owner-occupancy, see J. Kain and J. Quigley, "Housing Market Discrimination, Home Ownership and Savings Behavior," *American Economic Review*, June 1972, pp. 263-77.

Notes to Chapter 4
Determinants of Tenure Choice in a Single
Housing Market

1. S. Maisel, "Rates of Ownership, Mobility and Purchase," *Essays in Urban Land Economics* (Los Angeles: UCLA Real Estate Research Program, 1966); Daniel Fredland, *Residential Mobility and Tenure Choice*, Harvard University, Ph.D. thesis, 1970; D.S. Projector and G.S. Weiss, *Survey of Financial Characteristics of Consumers* (Washington, D.C.: Board of Governors of the Federal Reserve System, 1966); John Bossons, "Credit Rationing, Indivisibilities, Portfolio Balance Effects, and the Wealth Elasticity of the Demand for Housing," Toronto, University of Toronto, unpublished paper, 1973; J. Kain and J. Quigley, "Housing Market Discrimination, Home Ownership and Savings Behavior," *American Economic Review*, June 1972, pp. 263-77. The studies by Bossons and Projector and Weiss on the tenure choice-wealth relationship are not further discussed here since no wealth data for households in a single market is available.

2. J. Tarner in his "Occupational Migration Differentials," (*Social Forces*, Vol. 43) reported for inter-city moves that (1) Labor force members are more mobile than those not in the labor force, (2) of those in the labor force, those employed are more mobile than the employed, and (3) of employed males, professionals and semi-professionals are the most mobile, while craftsmen, foremen, kindred workers and operatives are the least mobile. The most complete description of intra-urban relocators is available from San Francisco data in Chapter 7 of J.F. Kain (ed.), *The NBER Urban Simulation Model, Vol. II Supporting Empirical Studies* (New York: National Bureau of Economic Research, 1971).

3. The concavity will also increase as the level of income rises. For a discussion and estimates of the magnitude of the federal tax advantages of homeownership see Henry Aaron, "Income Taxes and Housing," *American Economic Review*, December 1970, pp. 789-806.

4. For a critical evaluation of the advantages of homeownership for renters

at the lower end of the income distribution, see Marcuse, "Homeownership for the Poor," Washington, D.C., Urban Institute Working Paper No. 112-26, 1971.

5. The Pittsburgh SMSA also includes Washington and Beaver Counties; they are excluded because they are included by the Census in a different "county group" and because of their relatively small populations they are not individually identified. For a description of the User's Sample see U.S. Bureau of the Census *Public Use Samples of Basic Records from the 1970 Census* (Washington, D.C.: U.S. Government Printing Office, 1972).

6. A.S. Goldberger, *Econometric Theory* (New York: John Wiley and Sons, 1965), pp. 251-54.

7. For details see G.W. Ladd, "Linear Probability Functions and Discriminant Functions," *Econometrica* 34 (1966): 873-85.

8. The only estimates which have been at all successful in determining a tax subsidy elasticity of homeownership are those recently done by Franklin James. For all households combined he estimates the elasticity, through a clever linking of data from several sources, to be about −1.0. For details see his, "Income Taxes and Homeownership," Washington, D.C.: Urban Institute Working Paper, 5031-3, 1975.

9. This result differs from that reported by Kain-Quigley, "Housing Market Discrimination" on the basis of their study for St. Louis households in which they found no systematic differences between races after controlling for family types with additive dummy variables.

10. The main reference is K.E. and A.F. Taeuber, *Negroes in Cities* (New York: Antheneum Press, 1969). Segregation indices for 1970 are reported in A. Sorensen, K.E. Taeuber, and L.J. Hollingsworth, Jr., "Indices to Racial Residential Segregation for 109 Cities in The United States, 1940 to 1970," Madison, Institute for Research on Poverty, Discussion Paper 200-74, 1974. For a further description of racial segregation in Pittsburgh see A.B. Schnare and R. Struyk, "An Analysis of Ghetto Housing Prices Over Time," paper presented at The National Bureau of Economics Research Conference on Income and Wealth, May 1975; J.T. Darden, *Afro-Americans in Pittsburgh* (Lexington, Mass.: Lexington Books, D.C. Heath and Company, 1973); and A. Epstein, *The Negro Migrant in Pittsburgh* (New York: Arno Press and the New York Times, 1969; re-publication of 1916 monograph of same title by University of Pittsburgh).

11. A related point concerns the differential in annual costs for the same unit as a result of owning rather than renting. Shelton's widely accepted analysis indicates the "typical differential" to be 2 percent of the value of the unit, a substantial inducement for ownership. Peter Marcuse, "Homeownership for the Poor," on the other hand, has argued that the economic benefits to the poor of homeownership may be small indeed. If one accepts Marcuse's argument, then the advantages of ownership hinge on the capitalization of the future rental stream relative to the selling price of the unit. For the details of Shelton's argument see his, "The Costs of Renting Versus Owning a Home," *Land Economics*, 1968, pp. 59-72.

12. While we have no direct evidence on such restrictive practices, J.T. Darden (*Afro-Americans in Pittsburgh*) makes a pervasive case for their existence in Pittsburgh.

Notes to Chapter 5
Differences in Homeownership Among Metropolitan Areas

1. For a description of these data see U.S. Bureau of the Census, *1970 Census User's Guide*, Vol. I and II (Washington, D.C.: U.S. Government Printing Office, 1970). Where necessary these data were supplemented with that from the printed statistics in the *Metropolitan Housing Characteristics* reports for the individual areas.

2. This index which ranges from 0 to 100 is interpreted as "showing the minimum percentage of non-whites who would have to change the block on which they live in order to produce an unsegregated distribution." K.E. and H.F. Taeuber *Negroes in Cities* (New York: Antheneum Press, 1969) pp. 30-33. For a discussion of the main weakness of these measures, that of not clearly separating economic and social segregation, see R.E. Zelder, "Racial Segregation in the Urban Housing Markets," *Journal of Regional Science* 10 (1970): 93-105.

3. Stanley Masters, *Effect of Housing Segregation on Black-White Income Differentials* (Madison: The University of Wisconsin Institute for Research on Poverty, Discussion Paper 134-72, 1972).

4. J. Kain and J. Quigley, "Housing Market Discrimination, Home Ownership and Savings Behavior," *American Economic Review*, June 1972, pp. 263-77.

5. On this point see Sherman Maisel, J. Burnham, and J.S. Austin, "The Demand for Housing: A Comment," *Review of Economics and Statistics*, November 1966, pp. 410-13.

Notes to Chapter 6
Determinants of the Rate of Homeownership of Black Households Relative to White Households

1. Major references from this large literature which have left the issue unresolved are: R.F. Muth, *Cities and Housing* (Chicago: University of Chicago Press, 1969); Thomas King and Peter Mieszkowski, *An Estimate of Racial Discrimination in Rental Housing*, Cowles Foundation Discussion Paper No. 307 (New Haven: Cowles Foundation, February 1971); Victoria Lapham, "Do Blacks Pay More For Housing," *Journal of Political Economy*; J.F. Kain and J.M. Quigley, "Measuring the Value of Housing," *Journal of the American Statistical Association* 65 (June 1970); 512-19; A. Schnare and R. Struyk,

"Analysis of Ghetto Housing Prices Over Time," paper presented at the NBER Conference on Income and Wealth, May 1975.

2. For an excellent review of these studies see Bennett Harrison, *Urban Economic Development: Surburbanization, Minority Opportunity, and the Condition of the Central City* (Washington, D.C.: The Urban Institute, 1974).

3. The most noteworthy contribution is J.F. Kain and J.M. Quigley, "Housing Market Discrimination, Homeownership, and Savings Behavior," *American Economic Review*, June 1972, pp. 263-77.

4. For a review of the theoretical models of the relation between race and housing prices see A.B. Schnare, *Externalities, Segregation, and Housing Prices*, (Washington, D.C.: The Urban Institute, Paper 208-24, 1974).

5. For details see Tables 2a and 2b in Duran Bell, "Indebtedness in Black and White Families," *Journal of Urban Economies*, 1974, pp. 48-60.

6. The Kain-Quigley analysis has stimulated a good deal of additional research in this area. See, for example, J.F. McDonald, "Housing Market Discrimination, Homeownership and Savings Behavior: Comment," *American Economic Review*, 1974, pp. 225-31; and E.A. Roistacher and J.L. Goodman, Jr., "Race and Homeownership: Is Discrimination Disappearing?" *Economic Inquiry*, forthcoming.

7. The simple correlation of $(X_b - X_w)$ and market size is 0.514, significant at the 5 percent level. Other analysis, though, has not indicated a strong relationship between housing costs per se as measured in the BLS data and city size. See the Appendix to R. Struyk, "A Comparison of FHA and BLS Price Indices of Owner-Occupied Housing in Urban Areas," Washington, D.C., The Urban Institute, Working Paper 208-7, 1972. Also, the relative low level of significance of the market size variable is attributable in part to its −0.5 simple correlation with the fraction of units in single unit structures.

8. The restriction of blacks to central city locations is one form of the discrimination process hypothesis which Kain-Quigley support in explaining the non-income determined residual difference in black versus white ownership rates. The unattractiveness of central cities for homeowners is clear from the results of estimating hedonic indices for the value of owner-occupied units within metropolitan areas. Central city locations are generally discounted. See R. Struyk with S.A. Marshall, "Estimating the Value of Housing Services with the Census Users' Sample: Comparative Results for Five Areas," Washington, D.C., The Urban Institute, Working Paper 208-10, 1973.

9. This point was made by Milton Friedman in his *A Theory of the Consumption Function* (Princeton: Princeton University Press, 1957). For a discussion of job instability among various groups, see Robert E. Hall, "Turnover in the Labor Force," *Brookings Papers on Economic Activity*, 1972, pp. 709-64. Finally, we would be remiss not to note the recent evidence by Richard B. Freeman showing the substantially stronger educational and economic positions of young black men; see his, "Changes in the Labor Market for Black Americans, 1948-72," *Brookings Paper on Economic Activity*, 1973, pp. 67-132.

10. Table 72, U.S. Bureau of the Census, *Current Population Reports*, Series P-60, No. 85 (Washington, D.C.: U.S. Government Printing Office, 1972).

11. See, for example, U.S. Civil Rights Commission, *Mortgage Money: Who Gets It?* (Washington, D.C.: Clearinghouse Publication No. 48, 1974).

12. Duran Bell, "Indebtedness in Black and White Families," Table 6, p. 57.

13. For an excellent review of the evolution in FHA programs and practices see P.M. Greenston, C.D. MacRae, and C.I. Pedone, "The Effects of FHA Activity in Older, Urban, Declining Areas: A Review of Existing, Related Analysis," Washington, D.C., Urban Institute Paper 220-1, 1974. The vehicle for the implementation of the reduction in the neighborhood soundness criteria has been the Section 223(e) program. The default rate for this program has been extremely high, one suspects in large measure due to the pressure to insure a large number of properties quickly at the outset of the program. The other main factor in the defaults is that the loans are made to low income families in lower quality neighborhoods, neighborhoods in which capital depreciation removes much of the financial incentive for homeownership. Selected data on default rates are in U.S. Congress, Subcommittee of the Committee on Government Operations *Review of Federal Housing Administration*, Part 2, 93rd Congress (Washington, D.C.: U.S. Government Printing Office, 1974).

14. In his, "An Analysis of Discrimination by Real Estate Brokers," Madison, Institute for Research on Poverty Discussion Paper 252-75, 1975, Yinger also provides a good review of prior studies in this area.

15. See Chapter 4 of J.T. Darden, *Afro-Americans in Pittsburgh* (Lexington, Mass.: Lexington Books, D.C. Heath and Company, 1973).

16. This point has been made by Anthony Pascal in "The Analysis of Residential Segregation," in John Crecine (ed.), *Financing the Metropolis*, (Beverly Hills, Calif.: Sage Publications, 1970), pp. 401-34.

Notes to Chapter 7
Housing Allowances, Inflation, and Homeownership Rates

1. For a broad overview of the supply-side strategy see Chapter 4 of Dick Netzer, *Economics and Urban Problems* (New York: Basic Books, 1974). For a comprehensive discussion of the evolution of housing legislation, see Chapter 1 of U.S. Department of Housing and Urban Development, *Housing in the Seventies* (Washington, D.C.: U.S. Government Printing Office, 1974).

2. Of course, it is both possible and likely that non-participating households of the same income groups were receiving some indirect benefits from the programs. Chapter 4 of *Housing in the Seventies*, provides data on the rates of participation of eligible households by income class for several of the larger federal programs.

3. A general overview of housing allowance programs is provided in F. de

Leeuw, S.H. Leaman, and H. Blank *The Design of a Housing Allowance* (Washington, D.C.: The Urban Institute, Paper 112-25, 1970). Several other forms of housing allowances are described and analyzed in L. Ozanne, "Simulations of Housing Allowance Policies for U.S. Cities: 1960-1970," Washington, D.C., Urban Institute Working Paper, 216-3, 1974; and D. Carlton and J. Ferreira, "The Market Effects of Housing Allowance Payment Formulas," Cambridge, Joint Center for Urban Studies of M.I.T. and Harvard University, Working Paper 32, 1975.

4. A number of these administrative problems are discussed in M. Drury, H. Fried, J. Heinberg, and S. Kamm, "Direct Cash Assistance and Homeownership: The Issues," Washington, D.C., Urban Institute Working Paper 210-7, 1974.

5. This type of program was first sketched in E. Smolensky, "Public Housing or Income Supplements—the Economics of Housing the Poor," *Journal of American Institute of Planners*, 1968, pp. 94-101; it is also described and discussed in the references given in note 3 above.

6. The values used here are based generally on those for the 22 percent eligible program given in Chapter 6 of F. de Leeuw and R. Struyk, *The Web of Urban Housing* (Washington, D.C.: The Urban Institute, 1975); additional results for a similar program are given in L. Ozanne, "Simulations of Housing Allowance Policies."

7. The base year expenditures for households in each income class were based on the figures on house values for owner-occupants by income class and gross rents by income class found in Tables B-1 and B-2 of U.S. Bureau of the Census, *1970 Metropolitan Housing Characteristics*, Final Report HC(2)-1 (Washington, D.C.: U.S. Government Printing Office, 1972). House values were converted to rents using a rent-value ratio of 0.008; for the justification for this ratio see the final section of Chapter 2 of this volume.

8. There has been considerable controversy over what the value of the income elasticity of demand is. The upper value of the range of generally accepted estimates is 1.0, with values as low as 0.5 also being commonly held. Since the percentage change in income equals the percentage change in expenditures divided by the income elasticity of demand for housing services, use of a relatively high elasticity value will result in a relatively low percentage change in income, and thus a conservative estimate of the effect on homeownership rates. For a review of the elasticities controversy, see G. Carliner, "Income Elasticity of the Demand for Housing," *Review of Economics and Statistics*, 1973, pp. 528-32.

9. There is only fragmentary evidence available on the price elasticity of demand; but what there is suggests a value of about -1.0. See, for example, F. de Leeuw, "The Demand for Housing: A Review of the Cross-Section Evidence," *Review of Economics and Statistics*, 1971, pp. 1-10. The elasticity of substitution between land and capital in the production of housing also appears to be quite limited, with the range being 0.5 to 1.0. Estimates of the elasticity of

substitution are in R.F. Muth, "The Derived Demand for Residential Land," *Urban Studies*, 1971, pp. 243-54; and R. Koenker, "An Empirical Note on the Elasticity of Substitution Between Land and Capital in a Monocenter Housing Market," *Journal of Regional Science*, August 1972, pp. 299-306.

10. The discussion of the price indices is based heavily on Chapter 8 of U.S. Department of Housing and Urban Development *Housing in the Seventies*; and J. Weicher and J.C. Simonson, "Recent Trends in Housing Cost," *Journal of Economics and Business* 27 (1975): 177-185. For complete description of the price indices see H. Humes and B. Schiro, "The Rent Component of the Consumers' Price Index," Parts I and II, *Monthly Labor Review*, 1956, pp. 189-96 and pp. 442-46.

Notes to Appendix A
Joint Determination of Tenure Choice and
Housing Consumption Decisions of Individual
Households

1. See F. de Leeuw, "The Demand for Housing: A Review of the Evidence," *Review of Economics and Statistics*, 1971, pp. 1-10.

Notes to Appendix B
Income Tax Advantages of Homeownership

1. This description is based in part on that by Henry Aaron in his "Income Taxes and Housing," *American Economic Review*, 1970, pp. 789-806.

2. For evidence on this point see F. de Leeuw, "The Demand for Housing: A Review of the Cross-Section Evidence," *Review of Economics and Statistics*, 1971, pp. 1-10.

3. The assumption for B can be challenged on the basis of data from the Projector-Weiss study that the ratio of debt to value of the home vary systematically by age. Since, though, the bulk of households in this study are being stratified by age group the assumption of the invariance of B within samples can still be justified. D. Projector and S. Weiss, *Survey of Financial Characteristics of Consumers*, (Washington, D.C.: Board of Governors of the Federal Reserve System, 1966).

4. Henry Aaron, *Shelter and Subsidies* (Washington, D.C.: The Brookings Institution, 1972), and Aaron, "Income Taxes and Housing."

5. Internal Revenue Service, *Statistics of Income—1969, Individual Tax Returns* (Washington, D.C.: U.S. Government Printing Office, 1971), Table 2.1.

Notes to Appendix C
Estimation of Permanent Income

1. We employ the term "permanent income" in the same sense that Friedman originally conceived it: "the nonhuman wealth [the unit] owns; the personal attributes of the earners of the unit, such as their training, ability, personality; the attributes of the economic activity of the earners such as the occupation followed, the location of economic activity and so on." Milton Friedman, *A Theory of the Consumption Function* (New York: National Bureau of Economic Research, 1957), p. 21.

2. Exceptions to this rule in the study of housing expenditures are T.H. Lee, "Housing and Permanent Income: Tests Based on a Three-Year Reinterview Survey," *The Review of Economics and Statistics* 50 (1968), and Geoffrey Carliner, "Income Elasticity of Housing Demand," *Review of Economics and Statistics* 55 (1973), pp. 528-32.

3. For a full description see U.S. Bureau of the Census, *Public Use Samples of Basic Records from the 1970 Census* (Washington, D.C.: U.S. Government Printing Office, 1972).

4. An implicit but very important assumption made in estimating a joint human capital-labor force participation model concerns the relationship between income and labor force participation. In this methodology the relationship is seen as strictly linear, that is invariant with the level of income. In brief, the rate of substitution of work for leisure is assumed to be the same across all households of the same race.

A number of other economists faced with the problem of estimating permanent income given current income have developed several techniques for making the estimates. The method used here most closely resembles that employed by E. Kalacheck and F. Raines in estimating the potential wages of the poor based on their earnings characteristics (but not on their labor participation) in, "Labor Supply of Low Income Workers," in *Technical Studies of the President's Commission on Income Maintenance Programs* (Washington, D.C.: U.S. Government Printing Office, 1970), pp. 159-87. A method requiring substantially less effort, which uses mean incomes of households stratified by years of education and age of head of house, has been employed by J.F. Kain and J.M. Quigley in "Housing Market Discrimination, Homeownership, and Savings Behavior," *American Economic Review*, June 1972, pp. 263-77. This method and others have been suggested by R. Ramanathan in several articles; see, for example, his "Measuring Permanent Income of a Household: An Experiment in Methodology," *Journal of Political Economy*, January 1971, pp. 177-85.

5. For white-collar workers, their findings are consistent with ours, showing an inverted *U*. See A. Rees and G.P. Schultz, *Workers and Wages in an Urban Labor Market* (Chicago: University of Chicago Press, 1970), Chapters 7-9.

6. One could conceive, however, of using the four-year panel survey data developed by the Survey Research Center to do a short-period test of the utility of the method outlined here as well as other proposed procedures for determining permanent income. *A Panel Study of Income Dynamics* (Ann Arbor: Institute for Social Research, The University of Michigan, 1970, 1971). These data were used by Carliner, "Income Elasticity of Housing Demand," *Review of Economics and Statistics* 55, November 1973, pp. 528-32.

7. Definitions from "1970 Public Use Sample Users Dictionary," in U.S. Bureau of the Census, *Public Use Samples of Basic Records from the 1970 Census: Descriptions and Technical Documentation* (Washington, D.C.: U.S. Government Printing Office, 1972).

Notes to Appendix E
Notes on the Determinants of X_j

1. R.F. Muth, "Urban Residential Land and Housing Markets," in H.S. Perloff and Lowdon Wingo, Jr. (eds.), *Issues in Urban Economics* (Baltimore: The Johns Hopkins Press, 1968), p. 287.

2. These data are provided in Federal Housing Administration, *FHA Homes—1969* (Washington, D.C.: U.S. Government Printing Office, 1970), publication RR: 250 Book, HUD SOR-3. Data were not available for the SMSA for Cedar Rapids, Champaign-Urbana, Durham, Hartford, and Lancaster; for these the state average was used.

Index

Index

About the Authors

Raymond J. Struyk did his undergraduate work at Quincy College and received the doctorate in economics from Washington University in 1968. He has taught economics at Rutgers and Rice Universities. His research has been in the area of urban industry location and the economics of housing. He is coauthor of *Intrametropolitan Industrial Location: The Pattern and Process of Change* and *The Web of Urban Housing: Analyzing Policy With a Market Simulation Model.*

Sue Marshall received the B.A. in economics from Antioch College and is currently doing graduate work at the University of Maryland. For the past three years, she has been a member of the Housing Studies Group of The Urban Institute, where she has contributed to the publication of several articles and papers.